TO DO JUSTLY

A Junior Casebook for Social Action

KU-208-379

Association for Jewish Youth
Norwood House
Harmony Way
Off Victoria Road
London NW4 4BZ
Tel: 0181 203 3030
Fax: 0181 202 3030

One must repeat, from time to time: The world was created for my sake. Never say: What do I care about this or that? Do your part to add something new, to bring forth something that is needed, and to leave the world a little better because you were here briefly.

Rabbi Nachman of Bratzlav

TO DO JUSTLY

A Junior Casebook for Social Action

by ALBERT VORSPAN

Union of American Hebrew Congregations
New York

Library of Congress Catalog Card No. 79-92160

Second Revised Edition, 1978
COPYRIGHT 1969, © 1977

by UNION OF AMERICAN HEBREW CONGREGATIONS
838 FIFTH AVENUE   NEW YORK

    3   4   5   6   7   8   9   10

Produced in the United States of America

Editor's Introduction

When *To Do Justly* first appeared in 1969, it bore the legend "Experimental Edition." The editor and the author were not sure at the time whether sixth grade students in Jewish religious schools would be able and willing to confront the important social issues of contemporary society and relate them to Jewish values.

They need not have been concerned. Now in its seventh printing, *To Do Justly* has become a classic in Jewish social action literature. Albert Vorspan's genius for talking to young people in print has touched the lives of tens of thousands of students. Though the book's illustrative issues have changed with time, the Jewish insistence on a just and decent society, now as then, comes through as a powerful affirmation of faith and commitment.

This revised edition contains a great deal of new material—on religious cults, women's rights, Reform Judaism and Israel, anti-Semitism, and a host of other concerns. We know you'll find it a valuable addition to your school's classroom. And we hope it will bring young Jews even closer to the precious legacy of justice, given us in trust from the past—ours to preserve for the future.

Daniel B. Syme
National Director of Education

Preface

A famous British writer and scientist, C.P. Snow, once said that the Jewish people is a superior people because excellence is passed on through our genes. He said this is the only way to explain why the Jewish group, a tiny fraction of humanity, has contributed more than one-third of all the Nobel Prize winners of the world.

I agree with C.P. Snow that Jews are a remarkable people. We are not better, not worse, but we *are* different. I do not like theories of racial superiority and inferiority. Such ideas lead to dangerous prejudices and even persecution. And, of course, Mr. Snow is not a racist but was merely trying to understand why Jews are so devoted to education, so concerned with social justice and — as a group — so dedicated to liberal and humane ideals.

Where he went wrong, however, is in thinking that the secret of the Jews is in our genes. It is in our history, which is unique among all the peoples of the earth. The Exodus; the Ten Commandments at Sinai; our wandering through history; our suffering at the hands of Crusaders, popes, and kings; our stiff-necked insistence on living — these have left their mark on you and on me. They have given us depths of sympathy and feeling.

And the secret is to be found in our religion, our living faith of Judaism. Other religions concentrate on the world to come. Judaism cares about this world. Other religions stress belief — believe and you will be saved. Judaism is a way of life; its test of a man is not what he believes but how he lives, what he does, how he treats his fellow man. Other faiths say God is all-powerful; He alone will cure the problems of war, poverty, floods, injustice in His own good time. Judaism rejects passing the buck to God. Judaism teaches that we are co-workers with God and that our task is to improve the world *here* and *now!* Other faiths are hung up with the problem of individual sin — drinking, gambling, obscenity. Judaism lays its stress on social justice, knowing that no man can be without sin if the total society is violent, mean, cold to the poor and the different. Judaism is a call to moral action. It places on every Jew, young and old, an ancient burden: What doth the Lord require of us? Only "to do justly, to love mercy and to walk humbly with our God."

Young people today are searching for values to live by. They are lashing out at the phoniness of so much they see about them. Jewish youth are prominent among them. They want to see people love each other, respect each other, work together. They will not be satisfied with the old ways. The want change. They are sick of hate, selfishness, and war. This book is written in the hope that you will find that the religious values which have kept the Jewish people alive and deeply human for 3,000 years will also stiffen your spine, soften your heart, and inspire you to change the world for the better.

Judaism is not just a series of pretty Bible stories. It is a bold idea — one of the most radical in human history — of how a person, under God, can live like a human being. Such a Judaism did not die with the prophets of Old. It is as alive and timely as today's headline. The wisdom of our history and our tradition can help us — and mankind — to tackle today's evils of war and poverty, hate and violence. This book does not set down easy answers to these problems. There are no easy answers. This book is intended to help us to help God to complete the unfinished task of creation.

This book is dedicated to you, a Jewish young person, about whom our fathers said: "Old men shall dream dreams but thy youth shall see visions."

A. V.

Contents

TO DO JUSTLY

A Junior Casebook for Social Action

ASSOCIATION FOR JEWISH YOUTH
AJY HOUSE, 50 LINDLEY STREET
E1 3AX   Tel. 01-790 6407/8

1. Jews and Non-Jews: The Curse of Anti-Semitism

You stand in the courtyard in Paris jammed in among hundreds of wild and cheering Frenchmen. You are frightened by the hate which is so thick that you feel you can reach out and touch it with your hands. "Down with the Jews! Kill the Jewish traitor! Kill Dreyfus!" the mob shrieks. Who is on trial here, you ask yourself — one man or the Jewish people? You are an Austrian writer and, although you were born Jewish, it never seemed very important to you before. But something is happening to you at this moment, and you will never be the same again. You realize that *you* are on trial, *you* are being condemned, *you* and all the Jews of the world — for the "crime" of being a Jew. Anger boils within you. For a moment you clench your fists and want to lash out at their blind and stupid prejudice.

At that moment, there begins the slow, sad, muffled beat of the drums and a French captain marches slowly to the center of the yard. He is Alfred Dreyfus, accused by the government of treason, sentenced to Devil's Island for the rest of his life. A general approaches Dreyfus, reads out the sentence, and tears the captain's epaulets from his uniform. The agony in Dreyfus' eyes is as if they had torn out his heart.

The scene above took place in Paris on September 2, 1894. It was a turning point in French history — and also in Jewish history. For the Austrian journalist, whose life was changed by this event, was Theodor Herzl. This was Herzl's first personal contact with anti-Semitism (hatred of Jews). It shook him to the core of his being. It broke his faith that mankind was moving toward a brotherhood of all men. He knew that Dreyfus was innocent,* that he had been framed by evil officers to make him a scapegoat (someone to blame) for *their* misdeeds. The word "scapegoat" comes from the Bible. In biblical days, a goat was killed to atone for the sins of the people (Lev. 16:8, 16:10, and 16:26). The officers knew that they could whip up anti-Jewish feeling throughout France. And they were right. Herzl realized that neither he nor any other Jew could be safe so long as Jew-hatred lurked so near to the surface everywhere in the world. And he realized, too, that he could no longer go on with his own comfortable life as an Austrian writer as if nothing had happened. He promised himself, then and there, to devote the rest of his life to saving the Jewish people from the dangers of anti-Semitism and persecution.

But what could he do? How could he go about it? What would you have done if you had been Herzl? Wouldn't you first have to figure out *why* there was anti-Semitism? Why is it that Jews have been scapegoats for tyrants throughout history? How could the problem of anti-Semitism be solved?

Herzl's conclusion was that Jews would always be mistreated so long as they did not have a homeland of their own. He said Jews were a people without a land and that made them "abnormal" and misunderstood. He felt that if Jews had a homeland somewhere, Jews everywhere would be a normal people, like the Irish, Greeks, Italians, and other peoples who have connections to a motherland somewhere. Herzl created

---

*In 1906 all France and the world realized that Dreyfus had been unjustly accused and convicted. His name was cleared and he was given the Legion of Honor, one of France's highest awards.

4

modern Zionism, a program to establish a Jewish homeland in Palestine. Most people, including many Jews, thought he was mad. But he poured out his heart and his energies organizing a world Zionist movement, writing books about a Jewish state, and pleading with popes and presidents and kings to help win Jewish rights to Palestine. He died at the age of forty-three in 1904, but he planted the seed which bore fruit in 1948 when the State of Israel was born as one of the great Jewish miracles of all time. Before he died, he told those who laughed at his vision that there would be a Jewish state within fifty years. And when they scorned him as a dreamer, he replied: "If we will it, it is no dream." He was one of the greatest Jewish leaders of all times. When you visit Israel, you will stop at the beautiful Herzl Memorial and realize how one man with an idea can push back history and bring a dream to life.

But, important as Israel is for the Jewish people, did it accomplish all that Herzl predicted? Has Jew-hatred ended throughout the world — in the Arab countries, the Soviet Union, and even the United States? Can you give examples? It must be admitted that the fact of Israel gives pride and hope to Jews everywhere. But it does not spell the end of anti-Semitism. That curse still goes on. So we must look elsewhere to try to understand it and cure it.

Jews have always been the handiest scapegoat for tyrants to use to unite their people against a false enemy.

From Haman to Hitler, Jews often were selected to shift the anger of the people from their own rulers to the Jews. Adolph Hitler told the German people that they lost World War I because they were "stabbed in the back by the Jews," Joseph Stalin told the Russian people that their troubles were not caused by his harsh rule, or by the mistakes of communism, but by the "cosmopolitans" and "Zionists" — by which he meant Jews. Some Arab firebrands tell their people that their miserable, grinding poverty is the fault of "Zionist imperialism" — the Jews. And in communist Poland, when students demonstrated at the colleges for more freedom, the government commissars quickly pinned the blame on the "Zionists" — the Jews. The Polish case shows most keenly the cruelty of such scapegoating. There are only a few thousand Jews living in all of Poland — three million Polish Jews had been slaughtered by Hitler. It seems we can have anti-Semitism without Jews. After all the bloodshed and horror, Jews still seem to be the most convenient scapegoat that any bad ruler can come up with.

Why the Jews? One reason is that the ground was fully prepared for anti-Semitism more than 2,000 years ago. Although it was the Romans who crucified the Jew, Jesus, the New Testament (Christian Bible) blames the Jews for the murder of Jesus, whom Christians call Messiah and the son of God; Jews believe that there is only one God and that all men are the sons of God. But the charge of deicide (killing of God) was made against Jews through centuries of bloody persecution. It became the excuse for torturing Jews, trying to force them to convert to Christianity, putting Jews in ugly "ghettos" in Europe during the Middle Ages, burning them at the stake in the Spanish Inquisition, expelling them from almost every country in Europe, and blaming them to hide the ills of many nations. Even Hitler said Christian teaching had prepared the tinderbox for his persecution of Jews: all he had to do was put the torch to it.

Only in the last few years have Christian groups admitted the terrible wrongs against the Jews that have come from the teachings of the Christian Bible. They

6

now admit that it is wrong to teach that Jews killed Jesus. And now there is an effort by Christianity to correct the Sunday school books and parochial school texts so that the prejudice against Jews will no longer be planted in children's minds.

But religion is not the only root of anti-Semitism. There are many others. One has to do with money. When times are bad, and many people are without jobs and anxious about their future, anti-Semitism grows. There is also jealousy. Jews are hard-working, serious about education, good at business and professions. They have achieved much success in American life. There is bound to be envy on the part of those who have not made it, especially those who are not strong enough to admit their own failures. They excuse their failings by blaming others. What kind of people hate Jews? Studies show that those who are less-educated, those who do not feel secure about themselves, those who are angry about their lives, and those who hate people who are "different" become anti-Semitic most easily.

Since the beginning of history, people have always disliked those who are different from themselves — in color, religion, beliefs, even clothes, and hair dress. Haven't you ever wondered why adults get so upset when youngsters sprout long hair and beards? People resent whatever is different. Jews are different from other groups, and we insist upon our right to be ourselves. Do you think anti-Semitism would go away if Jews behaved more like non-Jews? What if we converted to Christianity? One thing we have learned is that anti-Semitism is a Gentile problem. There is not much that Jews can really do about it. If we try to change our behavior to please non-Jews, we will only give up our self-respect without in any way getting rid of the problem of anti-Semitism.

7

There have been many examples of this. In recent years the Ku Klux Klan has been active in the south in fighting against justice for the blacks. It has used bombings and other violence to scare people. It has used anti-Semitism by calling integration of blacks a "Jewish-Communist plot." This was done in communities where Jews were among the leaders in the fight for racial justice. And it was used equally where Jews were silent and played no part. What does this prove? Should Jews stand up for what is right or should we listen to those among us who warn us not to stick our necks out because it will cause anti-Semitism?

There are Jews who ask: After all our suffering, why should we still keep up a separate religion? Especially since the other faiths and the western world have all accepted the most important ideas about God and man and justice? Why be different? Wouldn't it be better if there were one religion for all the world instead of hundreds of different ones? What would you answer to these questions?

There are many answers. It is true that the Jewish religion gave the world some of its most important ideas — one God, the idea of human brotherhood, equality, justice, and peace. But Judaism, for the Jew, has many truths in it that can help us make the right choices in life. Judaism is not the same as any other religion. Just to show one example: Christianity is based on what a person believes (believe in Jesus and you will be saved). Judaism teaches that what you *believe* is not as important as what you *do* in life. Christianity teaches that the Messiah has come in the form of Jesus; we Reform Jews believe that no Messiah will come but that all of us together, as copartners with God, can bring about the Messianic Age of real peace and justice among all men.

8

Even on certain problems of our own day, there are deep differences among religions. We are not alike. Catholics, for example, are taught that divorce is a sin and that married couples have no right to divorce for any reason. Jews regard divorce as something necessary when a marriage fails. It is not that Catholics are wrong and Jews are right or vice versa. These views come from deep and honest religious ideas which are different. The important thing is for each religion to teach its own ideas and to respect the differing ideas of other religions. The only way to get all men to have one religion is to use force. And that is no longer religion — it is slavery. Just as the world will find peace only when communism and democracy and other systems learn to live together with respect and without forcing their ways on others, so in the world of religion. Mankind is richer with an orchestra of different religions, striking different notes and using different instruments rather than trying to turn the world into one dull key. Differences in religions, nationalities, and ethnic groups should be enjoyed and kept alive. They make life more interesting and more human.

Jews believe that it is helpful to educate all people to the evils of prejudice and anti-Semitism. This can be done through books, school, movies (have you ever seen a movie about anti-Semitism? There have been many good ones), and television. But the best way to fight anti-Semitism is to make sure that America is a healthy country. This is one reason Jews work so hard to bring justice to the black, to get rid of slums and poverty, to keep our cities from dying, to build decent housing for all Americans, and to see that everybody has a job and a fair chance at a good life. When the society is healthy, Jews are safe. When a society is unjust and tense and treats any of its citizens as second-class people, Jews are not safe. A truly fair and open America is the best weapon against anti-Semitism.

Anti-Semitism was not a serious problem for American Jews until the early part of the twentieth century. In the 1920's prejudice against Jews was a powerful factor in the Ku Klux Klan, which once was a strong force in many northern states, as well as in the south. Anti-Semitism then cut down the opportunities of Jews for good jobs, education, and housing. There were quotas (percentages) for Jews in colleges, and they were kept out of many professions, businesses, and neighborhoods. Such Jewish defense agencies as the American Jewish Committee, Anti-Defamation League, and American Jewish Congress were organized to work against persecution of Jews overseas as well as the mounting hatred in the United States. A danger point in anti-Semitism in the United States came in 1913 with the lynching of a Jew, Leo Frank, in Georgia after a false charge of murder. In the 1920's the publication of Henry Ford's *Dearborn Independent,* an anti-Semitic journal filled with wild reports of an international Jewish conspiracy, spread the poison. During the Depression came Father Coughlin's anti-Semitic radio program, spewing hatred against Jews over the radio network to millions of Americans. In the 1930's, under the pressure of the Depression in the United States and the rise of Nazism in Europe, anti-Semitism became a serious menace to Jewish security in America. Respectable political figures lent themselves to anti-Semitic movements. Nazi brownshirters paraded on the streets of New York. Anti-Semitism was widespread, open, and a clear and present danger to American Jewry and to America itself.

The situation changed rapidly — and for the better —

10

after World War II. The nation's struggle against Hitlerism made anti-Semitism a hated thing to most Americans. Jews gained free access to jobs, housing, and colleges. Anti-Semitism backfired as a political tool. No respectable public figure would touch it. Open anti-Semitism almost disappeared, although anti-Jewish feeling from time to time still bubbles up as in the controversy over black rights. The number of anti-Semitic organizations and publications reached a very low ebb after the war. Jews gained a greater sense of security. Indeed, Jewish defense agencies felt free to devote the bulk of their energies and resources to working for black rights and other general American problems. With quotas and barriers against Jews largely swept aside, Jews flocked into the professions. By 1967, Jews were one of the best educated and economically most successful religious groups in American life.

Yet, even in America, anti-Semitism does not die. If you read the newspaper or watch the news on television, you know that there have been some recent public expressions of anti-Semitism in America. No doubt you have also heard your parents discuss these problems. Can you give an example of a recent incident of anti-Semitism?

There have been some ugly examples of anti-Semitism in American life in recent years. The chairman of the Joint Chiefs of Staff — General George Brown — made a speech in which he said that Jews own the banks, the newspapers, and the television in the United States and that the "Jewish lobby" in behalf of Israel really runs the Congress. What do you think about such a speech? Is it true? What should the Jewish people have done to react to General Brown? Was his speech anti-Semitic?

Jewish groups were furious about Brown's remarks.

11

They sent telegrams to the President, protesting the fact that the highest ranking general was spouting such anti-Jewish poison. They pointed out that Brown's statements were nonsense, that they spread hatred among the American people, and that no bigot should be head of the Joint Chiefs of Staff. President Ford — and later President Carter — spoke out against General Brown's statements, but they did not agree to fire him. After a while, the Jewish groups gave up the fight and let the matter die down. Some Jews were bitter, arguing that no prejudiced person — whether anti-Jewish, anti-black, anti-Catholic, or whatever — should be allowed to stay in high public office, representing all of the people. What do you think? On the other side of the coin, some other Jews said that if Jewish protest could get General Brown fired it would only show that Jews have as much power as Brown claimed they have. What are your thoughts?

Anti-Semitism also got a big push by virtue of the propaganda campaign of the Arabs. Backed by billions of petrodollars, the Arabs put out a propaganda and advertising campaign against the "Zionists." They used the dreadful resolution which they put through the United Nations, calling Zionism (do you remember what Zionism is? See page 4) a form of racism. The Arabs also organized a boycott against American businesses which do any trade with Israel and also against firms in which "Zionists" play a part. This is illegal and un-American, and the government of the United States took steps in 1977 to stop it. But anti-Jewish hatred continued to be pumped out on college campuses, in slick advertising campaigns, and in whispering campaigns repeating the kind of lies dished out by General Brown.

How can Jews defend themselves against such attacks? Remember that free speech also protects hate-mongers, so there is not too much that can be done, ex-

12

cept to answer with the truth and to expose the lies, trusting the American people to make a fair judgment.

Is the American people fair? In general, yes. Of course, there are people who have false ideas about Jews. But, in general, the American people is very sympathetic to Israel and to the Jewish people. That is why — and not because of a lobby in Washington — the Congress gives large military and economic support to Israel. When the Arabs blackmailed us with their oil embargo in 1973, they tried to blame Israel for the discomfort we Americans had to face with high gas prices and long lines at the gas stations. But the Americans didn't buy it. We were angry at the Arabs for putting a gun at our heads. A few bigots put ugly bumper stickers — "BURN JEWS, NOT OIL" — on their cars, but most Americans were decent and understanding and didn't scapegoat Israel or Jews. That was a good sign.

Similarly, in 1976, when Jimmy Carter was elected (with strong support from Jewish voters), there was little anti-Semitism in the political campaigns. Indeed, two additional Jewish senators were elected in 1976. One was Howard Metzenbaum of Ohio; the other was Edward Zorinsky of Nebraska. Both are good Jews, active in Jewish affairs and their synagogues. Metzenbaum had been chairman of the national Commission on Social Action of Reform Judaism. Both ran in conservative states where Jewish voters made up only a small fraction of the voters. Yet they were elected. If anti-Jewish feeling was strong in America, could such men — with such Jewish-sounding names and backgrounds — be elected? Obviously not. That, too, was a good sign.

Yet anti-Semitism is never too far from the surface in any country. If a nation has bad times — say, a depression, with millions of people out of work and angry — there is always a danger that the people will lash out at one minority or another. Jews are never safe in an angry country. This is why we must always work for just and decent conditions for all people ... certainly *one* reason.

There are many young people who are sincerely working for basic changes in America to bring an end to wars like Vietnam, to bring more justice to blacks and to poor people in our midst. But there are some youngsters and older people, too, who believe that America is a rotten, or fascist, or evil society and that the only way to bring justice is to tear down the system by force. Some of these young people have caused bloody riots on some college campuses. They are as wrong as the people on the extreme right, and they, too, are looking for scapegoats and simple answers. The truth is that the only way to bring real change and progress to America is, as it has always been, by working through legal and democratic means, by electing good people and working for good laws. Violence from the extremists on one side only strengthens the extremists on the other side. Each excess from violent rebels brings thousands more people to believe in people like Wallace who promise to bring law and order at the end of a policeman's night stick.

Some of these young revolutionaries are anti-Semitic. They believe that America is a wicked society and that all the countries allied with America are on the wrong side of the world struggle. Since Israel is an ally of the United States, these young people conclude that Israel is also a wicked capitalist state. They put a halo on Israel's Arab neighbors and call these aggressive and backward Arab states "peace-loving, socialist states." You then have the weird situation in which the only democracy in that part of the world — Israel — is seen as bad, while such corrupt, feudal regimes as Saudi Arabia (which just got around to abolishing slavery but which still has public torture), Iraq (where mobs celebrate public hangings as if they were carnivals), and Egypt are seen as good countries. What is even more strange is that some of the American revolutionaries who have swallowed this childish propaganda are Jews! How can you explain it?

There is another kind of anti-Semitism which is causing more pain to Jews than the kinds already described. It is the anti-Semitism being expressed by some black people in America. Have you heard or read anything about this? Can you give an example?

This kind of anti-Semitism is more painful to Jews because we Jews have worked side by side with black people for their rights in America. So it comes as a shock when some black militants use anti-Semitism to fight their battles. In New York City, in 1968, there was a teachers' strike in which all the schools in the city were closed down for several weeks. Since most of the teachers in New York City are Jewish, some blacks blamed the strike on "Jew teachers." Is that anti-Semitism or not? Why? One of the terrible problems in America is that black children in slum areas do not receive a good education. They fall further behind every year in reading and writing. Some black militants in New York City said this was because of a "Jewish plot" to "poison the minds of black people." Another black said that Hitler didn't kill enough Jews. Still another read a poem on the radio which said, "You Jew, with your yarmalke, I wish you were dead."

Most black people — and most white people, too — are not anti-Semites. Some angry young black militants, angry at their continued poverty and misery, are lashing out at the white society. Some lash out at what they refer to as "Jew slum landlords" who, they say, take advantage of black people in the black ghettos. What do

15

you think causes such attitudes? Is it fair to call some-body a Jew landlord? Isn't it fairer to condemn him for what he does wrong as a landlord (who happens to be Jewish) than to condemn him as a Jew?

What should Jews do about black anti-Semitism? The answer is that we should do exactly the same as we do against white anti-Semitism. We should speak out against bigotry whether it comes from blacks or from whites. We should ask black leaders to speak out against hatred. We should point out that hatred is like a boome-rang; it circles back and hurts the person who uses it. But we also must be very careful not to exaggerate the amount of black anti-Semitism. Why do we get more excited about black anti-Semitism than white? We have to be very careful not to get so angry and excited about these incidents that we blame the whole black race for it. It would be as unfair to call all blacks anti-Semitic as it would be to call all Jews racists because a few Jews are anti-black. You cannot blame an entire group for the deeds of a few. That is stereotyping, putting a label on a whole group. And, above all else, we have to remember that we Jews must continue to work for justice for all people and for a better America and a peaceful world. The best way to fight anti-Semitism is to solve the social problems — slums, ignorance, racial injustice, un-employment — which breed hatred and scapegoating and bigotry. Each human being should be judged on his merit as an individual and not by some group label.

Projects

1. All these discussions have raised some basic questions. One is: Does Christianity and its teachings — that the Jews are damned for killing Jesus — contribute to anti-Semitism?

16

As you know, this was one of the key issues before the Roman Catholic Church at the Vatican Council. A subcommittee of the class should research this subject and prepare a report for the full class. Read Chapter X of *Justice and Judaism*, by Albert Vorspan and Rabbi Eugene J. Lipman (New York: Union of American Hebrew Congregations, 1959). Write to the Department of Interfaith Activities, Union of American Hebrew Congregations, 838 Fifth Avenue, New York, New York 10021. Talk to a local Catholic priest and Protestant minister to see what they say about this problem. Also, find out what is being done in *your* school to teach understanding of non-Jewish religions. What is being done in your community to improve interreligious relations?

2. Imagine that you are on the Board of Temple Isaiah in a large metropolitan city. A young "black power" leader, Bob Green, has been all over the front pages attacking Mr. Rittenhotter, who is a member of your synagogue, as a "Jew slumlord, gouging and exploiting black people in the slum." The president of the synagogue asks what should be done. Should we call Green an anti-Semite? Should we meet with him and try to show him that mistreating people is not just a Jewish question, but a community problem? Should we ignore it? And what about Rittenhotter? If he is exploiting people, is it a proper concern of the synagogue to take some action? After all, people of all backgrounds sometimes exploit blacks, including fellow blacks! Should the rabbi meet with him to persuade him to correct his conduct? Is what he is doing against Judaism? If so, do we have a right to expel him from membership? Or would that be wrong? Or do we take the position that Jews are entitled to their share of bad people, too, and that we cannot take responsibility for individual Jews as a Jewish community? Let's decide!

3. What are the chief causes of anti-Semitism? And how can these causes be dealt with? Read "The Faces of Anti-Semitism," a pamphlet by the American Jewish Committee, 165 East 56 Street, New York, N.Y. 10022.

4. Have you ever come across anti-Semitism yourself? What would you do if you did? Imagine that a classmate of yours in public school walks home with you one day and says: "You Jews are all stuck-up, you think you're better than anybody else." Is that an anti-Semitic statement or not? And how would you respond? Designate one member of the class to

be your non-Jewish classmate and one to be you.

5. There are some people who think that you cannot change the mind of a bigot. Do you agree with that? These people say it is a waste of breath to try to answer a bigot because he will not listen to facts. However, they say it is important to answer a bigot when other people are around so that they will not be poisoned by bigotry. Imagine you are an adult on a bus and a noisy passenger yells out, as the bus passes New York University in New York City, *"Hey, there's New York Jew-niversity."* A few people snicker. Most people are silent. What do you say? Assign the roles to members of the class: the bigot, you, other passengers, the driver. Is it worthwhile to respond to him or should you ignore him? If you are silent, won't you hate yourself afterward? Which of the following responses seems wisest?

    (a) Ignore him.
    (b) Shame him with a sarcastic answer.
    (c) Ask the bus driver to remove him.
    (d) Demand an apology.
    (e) Ignore him but speak to the other
passengers to explain the evil of bigotry.

6. There are hundreds of country clubs which will not admit Jews as members. Do you think they have a right to keep Jews (or blacks or other groups) out? Jews have organized their own country clubs in most of these towns. Is this better than fighting the discrimination of the other clubs?

7. Invite a representative of the American Jewish Committee or Anti-Defamation League to visit the class and talk about anti-Semitism in your town.

8. Show one of the following movies:

    (a) *Anti-Semitism in America.* ADL (Anti-Defamation League).

    (b) *The High Wall.* The disease of prejudice. ADL.

    (c) *Picture in Your Mind.* A provocative cartoon on roots of prejudice. ADL.

9. Would anti-Semitism disappear if the Jews were like everybody else? If Jews were mostly farmers and laborers? If we gave up our religion?

10. Could a Jew be an anti-Semite?

2. Equal Rights

One day Larry came home from school, tossed his books (as usual) on the kitchen table, and started to race out the door to play ball with his friends. His mother stopped him (as usual) and made him take the books up to his room.

"What happened at school today?" she asked later, giving him a cookie.

"Nothing," he muttered through the straw in his chocolate milk.

"Oh, Larry, *something* must have happened."

"Oh, yeah," Larry said, "our teacher wasn't there today. She was sick or something."

"Then, who taught your class?"

"A maid," Larry said, slipping out of the door.

A maid? What did Larry mean? Why did he think that the substitute teacher was a maid? Do you think this story took place in a suburb or in the city? Why?

The story about the maid shows one of the biggest problems in America. It is not just that black people in America are not yet free. It is also that white people do not really know blacks. We only know them as our maids, or handymen, or as people who work for our fathers. We think of them as one group, but we do not know them as friends, as real people. This is why it is so hard for us to understand what black people are facing. We see the riots on television. We read the headlines. We hear about all the trouble, and we get scared. We just wish they would stop. But who are "they?" There is no "they." There are millions of separate human beings — each with his own dreams, fears, and hopes. It is hard for white people to really feel the pain which black Americans feel. To understand will require from each of us an ability to feel ourselves into the very skin of our black fellow Americans. It may not be possible, but we must try.

One white American writer actually had his skin treated so that it was black for a few weeks. (Did you see the movie, "Black Like Me"? It's also a book by John Howard Griffin.) He did this so he could live among blacks and feel what their life is like. Does it take such drastic action? Many people feel that America is really two separate nations — two different Americas. They say we whites only really notice the blacks when one of our cities goes up in flames.

Usually, the black person is invisible to us. He lives on the other side of town, trapped in a slum he cannot escape. Do you know what a ghetto is? The word comes from the situation of Jews in Europe when they had to live in separate, often walled-in, places. They could not leave their towns (ghettos) without special permission. Jews, therefore, should know the evil of a ghetto. Let us try, by using our imagination, to pierce the world of the black, to put ourselves into the skin of another American, to "understand the heart of the stranger," for he, like us, is a child of God. And he, like us, needs to be seen and heard and understood.

... Pretend you are Cazzie Hollis. You are eleven years old and you are black. Your real name is Stanley, but everybody calls you Cazzie because your idol is Cazzie Russell, the former basketball star of the New York Knicks. Sometimes, at night, you dream that you are a famous athlete, like Cazzie, dunking a shot in the last second of play while the crowd in Madison Square

Garden is on its feet shouting itself hoarse for you. But, really, you don't believe you will ever make it. You really don't think you'll ever make it out of Harlem. You are eleven years old and you have been outside of Harlem only twice in your life. Once to visit a relative in South Jamaica. Once when your uncle took you to the beach at Coney Island. You've never even been to Madison Square Garden to see Cazzie. Your family can't afford such things. You've only seen him on television. Your world is very small, all black, and full of traps, but you don't understand that. It's the only world you've ever known.

You live with your two brothers, sister, mother, and grandmother in a two-room apartment in an old, crumbling building. You never knew your father. Mom told you he died when you were a baby, but your older brother, Leroy, has told you "he just ran off when we were young because he couldn't support us and he was plain ashamed." Mom works as a maid for a white family on Long Island, and she is gone when your grandma wakes you up for school in the morning. You and your brothers sleep in one bed. Sometimes, when you watch television and see the homes the whites live in, you imagine yourself with a room of your own, with pictures and pennants on the wall, and a big bed of your very own. But you don't really believe that will happen either. People on welfare don't live like the whites on television. You already know that it is good to be white and bad to be black. Once you told Leroy that you wished you had been born white instead of black. He slapped you hard across the face. "It's bad enough they hate you. Don't hate yourself. Black is beautiful, boy, don't you ever forget it!"

You don't like school. The school building is 117 years

21

old, and it stinks even worse than your apartment building. All the students in school are black or Puerto Rican. Most of the teachers are white. Your books are almost as old as you are, and they are falling apart. You have learned about Lincoln, Jefferson, the Mayflower, but they never teach you about *your* forefathers. Weren't your people here before anybody else except the Indians? How come there are no black faces in your books? Many of your teachers don't seem to like teaching black kids. They act like you're all dumb and the best thing to do with you is try to keep you quiet. You told one teacher that you want to go to college and be a basketball player when you grow up. He laughed and said: "You forget about college, Stanley. You kids should be more realistic. Now being an athlete, that's a different story. You coloreds make good athletes. You've got a natural rhythm." Leroy dropped out of school when he was fifteen. You wonder if you will drop out, too.

You hate your apartment building, especially in the summer. There is no place to be alone even for a minute. Everybody's hollering, especially when it gets hot. The landlord never seems to come around except to collect the rent. Once, when a water pipe burst, the water poured all over the apartment for fourteen hours before the super finally sent a plumber. Mom cusses out the landlord and she is always calling up the Welfare and the City and complaining, but nothing is ever done about it. When your kid sister got bitten by a rat while she slept, your mom got so mad she went down and woke up the super in the middle of the night. But what can he do? He says the *Man* doesn't want to put more money into this dump, and that you can just move if you don't like it. But where could you move to? Your older brother once was reading the newspaper and he suddenly started

22

smashing his fist against the wall: "They found some rats down on Park Avenue and 67th Street and the City falls over itself to get those rats cleaned out that same day. How come they don't do that up here in Harlem? You want to know why, boy? We're black, boy! Just remember that!"

You love to read *Ebony* magazine which is like *Life*, only about blacks. You read about black athletes, black politicians like Senator Brooke, movie stars like Sidney Poitier, athletes like Cazzie Russell, O. J. Simpson, and Julius Erving. They live in beautiful houses, with green grass and back yards, and have automobiles and color television. Some live in white neighborhoods and have white maids, and they talk up integration and progress. But, to you, it's a dream world, like a movie. Your family has no part in it. When you go out on the street, you see the dope addicts, the pushers, and the hustlers and you don't like it. Sometimes a cop comes by and he says "Move on, nigger boy." And when you go shopping with mom, you see the way the white merchants palm off their shoddy stuff at prices your mother says are higher than they are in the fancy white shops downtown. Sometimes you get just plain mad. Your older brother says: "Cazzie, the system is rigged against us. We're in a black cage here, and integration is only for the birds who can fly to the suburbs. The only way out is to fight your way out." Mom fears that your brother is a member of the violent Black Panthers and she is scared every time he leaves the house.

Does all this talk about equality and justice and integration really mean anything? How come every good friend of the black man gets gunned down? How come Martin Luther King was killed? And Malcolm X? And the Kennedys? How come the people in Washington pass

23

laws and rulings for black people and nothing changes for you and your family? Is it all a lousy joke the whites play on you? Is Leroy right? If you work your tail off in school, will it do any good? Are your kids and their kids going to live in this meanness forever? For another 300 years? Sometimes you get so down you just don't talk to anybody. Sometimes you want to shout, to hit back, and to smash the whole ugly scene down.

Last week, on a muggy night, police sirens suddenly howled in the neighborhood. Windows smashed. People began to yell and run every which way. It was a *riot!* You were scared and excited, and your heart pounded just like the time Cazzie made a three-point play in the closing seconds of a play-off game. Then, you were *in* it. A gang smashed the window of a white television store. You ran, too, and you grabbed a small transistor radio. Why did you do it? You don't know, but you have to admit to yourself: *You're not sorry.*

For several years, America was aflame with riots and burning like this. Blacks were enraged, felt themselves cheated, lost faith in peaceful change. Now that chapter has passed. Blacks have returned to the political process to get their rights. More than any group, they were responsible for Jimmy Carter's election, and they have a right to expect laws which will gain jobs for unemployed people — including black youths, 40 per cent of whom were out of school and out of work in some cities — as well as a fair share of medical care, housing, education, and more humane welfare programs. Is there a better way to get rid of the anger and bitterness that led to violence and riots in the streets and burned down many neighborhoods?

But there are many other questions. Why is it you don't know Cazzie — or anyone like him? Why doesn't he

24

live in your neighborhood? Why doesn't he go to your school? The answer is that practically all the Cazzies are kept in another world, almost out of our sight. Few have the money to move out of their black slums. If they do have the money, they have a hard time getting a place to live in white neighborhoods. Even though it is against the law to discriminate (to keep someone out because of his color or religion), white people are usually afraid to sell or rent to blacks. Why do you think this is? Is it because they think their neighbors won't like it? Is it because they think it would lower the value of the houses in the neighborhood? The answer is yes. But it is also because most white people feel they are superior to blacks. This feeling is called racism. It is evil. It is the feeling which Hitler and his Nazis had about Jews.

So, Cazzie — and the millions like him — get stuck in ugly, rotten slums. They go to black schools which are very bad. The buildings are usually old and decaying. The books are beaten-up hand-me-downs. The classes are too big for individual attention. Very often the teachers, mainly white, are so worn out that they give up inside themselves and decide that black students just can't learn. When the teacher feels that way, she can't teach. Angry and upset, some of the black kids act up in class, and the teacher spends more time on discipline than on teaching. So each year the students in black slum schools fall further behind in the basic reading, writing, and arithmetic. In some black schools, four out of five kids drop out before they finish high school. When they drop out, most of them do not have the education to get a job, so they hang around the streets. Many get into trouble. In most cases, they have already dropped out of life. They have had it.

If all men are born equal, why should Cazzie have to go

to a school like his, while you go to modern, progressive schools? The public spends about $1000 a year to give a child in the suburbs the best education possible and to prepare him for life. Everyone assumes these children will go on to college; and 90 per cent of Jewish youngsters do. Less than $400 a year is spent by the public on Cazzie's education. It will be a miracle if he goes to college. But doesn't Cazzie need even better schools and teachers than we do to make up for his poor home life? What's wrong?

Black people are caught in a trap in our country. Most black men do not have the education to get decent jobs. But, as we get more and more automation, there is less and less chance for people without skills to find work. And even some well-educated black people, sometimes even those with doctorates, are kept out of good jobs because of their color; sometimes they wind up as janitors and dishwashers. While 5 per cent of the adult males can't find jobs in America, sometimes 30 per cent of the black men in the big cities are without any job at all. They and their families have to go on welfare — the government gives them a small pittance each month to keep the family fed and housed. Can you imagine what that does to the spirit of a man? Especially if his wife, working as a maid, becomes the main breadwinner of the family? Like Cazzie's father, many black men can't take the shame of it. They disappear, leaving the family to be raised by the mother. Or they get into trouble with the police. What do you think it does to a child to grow up without a father — or with a father he can't respect or try to be like?

One of the most important things that this treatment does to a black person is to make him dislike himself. There was once a test in which young black girls were asked to pick the doll they wanted from a wide choice of colors — jet black, brown, light brown, white. Almost every black girl picked a white doll. Can you figure out why? It is because America drums it into their heads that white is good, black is bad. These girls were ashamed of their blackness. Anybody who is constantly mistreated begins, sooner or later, to blame himself, and to be ashamed. (Jews have had the same experience in the past; only a generation ago some Jews hated themselves and changed their noses and/or their names.) The problem for the black then is also how he thinks of himself. He must build pride in his own race and background. He must respect himself because you cannot love and respect others until you respect yourself. He must stop straightening out his hair or bleaching his skin to try to be like the whites. He must have a sense of group pride, as Jews do, and a sense of responsibility to his race. This need is what is behind the black drive for "black power" and the slogan "Black Is Beautiful."

The result of all this — lack of jobs, bad schools, slum housing, poor family life — is that millions of black children are being hurt. They are not being killed by a gun or a poison, but their desire and hope and spirit are being killed. Many sink into not caring. Some others build up an anger at white society that is so powerful it leads to hatred and violence and to the idea of a separate black society, like a little Africa, right here in America. Does this make sense? Could it work?

The only hope for America is to develop a really integrated society. Integration means blacks and whites working and living together, not separately. Actually, a lot has been done to move toward this goal. The Supreme Court has ruled that racial segregation (keeping people separate because of their color) is against the law. The

Congress has passed laws to give every American the right to live wherever he can afford to live. Efforts are being made to improve black schools. The government is trying to train and find jobs for the hard-core poor. But all of this just scratches the surface. The fact is that 40 per cent of black people are below the poverty line, which means a family of four earns less than $5,850 a year. Could your family live on that? Blacks make up another America that has little in common with the rest of us. We do not know each other, so we are full of fear on both sides. The fact is that they are angry and have run out of patience waiting for America to keep its promises about equal opportunity and justice for all. What is to be done? There are really only two choices. Keep the black down by force, or lift up the black and build an integrated America in the suburbs, the cities, the schools, the factories, and everywhere.

Integration can work. Until 1948, professional baseball had a color line. Only whites could play in the big leagues. Everybody said that if a black man were to play, there would be terrible trouble among the players, the fans, and the teams. Branch Rickey, then owner of the Brooklyn Dodgers, cut through all this fear and hired Jackie Robinson to play second base for the Dodgers. There was some minor trouble. Some southern players baited Jackie. Some fans jeered. Some hotels, at first, refused to put the black player up. But Jackie quickly earned everyone's respect by the way he handled himself on and off the field. He was the pioneer. After that it was easy. Can you imagine professional baseball today without blacks?

The same thing happened in our armed forces. It is hard to realize that even as late as World War II, when we were fighting against Hitler's ideas of racial superiority, our armed forces were segregated. Everyone said you can't mix blacks and whites, it would cause conflict and tension. In 1948, President Truman didn't listen to the voices of habit and fear. He ordered the armed forces integrated. And the grumbling soon died away. The courage of black soldiers spoke more loudly than the prejudice of the ignorant. In the Vietnam war, black and white Americans fought side by side. More than 30 per cent of American troops were black; almost 50 per cent of the casualties were also black. The Vietnam war was a disaster in almost every way. But it proves that integration of the races is not only fair—it also works! Sadly, many of the black soldiers, returning home, learned the bitter truth that our army in Vietnam was more integrated than the America they had risked their lives for and now returned to. How do you think these men felt? How would you feel?

Usually, when we talk about racial justice, we think about doing the right thing for the sake of the blacks. That is important. But we have to do it for ourselves, too. We white people are also cheated by racial injustice. Can you think of how? In the first place, we do not have a chance to get to know and to live with people of other colors and backgrounds. Yet two-thirds of the people of the world are non-white, and we must learn how to live in a mixed world. Aren't we also deprived of a chance to know the real world? Second, studies show that white people in white suburbs come to think of themselves as superior to the poor and the black, and this kind of thinking is evil. Third, we must see that America — and, therefore, each of us — has no future if we cannot solve the racial problem which is today tearing apart the very fabric of American life. Riots and violence and hatred can destroy America. The only way to save America is to make it whole, to give every American a real chance at a decent life. We whites will have to make some sacrifices to do that. But, if we don't, we will grow up in a dangerous armed camp or in a country which keeps the races apart by force, like the Union of South Africa. We are a free country, and we must find ways to solve our problems in a free and just way. The fate of each of us — not only our black neighbors — depends on that. If blacks are not free, we whites cannot be free either.

As Jews, we have still another reason to work for racial justice. Our religion first gave the world the idea of the Fatherhood of God and the brotherhood of all men. Our fathers taught the world that every person is a child of God and must be regarded as precious. Jews taught that, when God created Adam, He fashioned him out of the clay of all colors and from all parts of the earth so that no man could ever say that "my people are better than yours." Democracy is based on the Jewish idea that every human being must be treated as the creature of God and given equal dignity, no matter his color or religion. "Love thy neighbor as thyself" is the first rule of Judaism.

We Jews were slaves in Egypt and we remind each other every Passover to "understand the heart of the stranger." The black man, who came to America before we did, is still "the stranger" in America. We Jews, who have been hurt by the haters and bullies of every generation and every land, must be among the first to stand up and be counted in the fight for justice for Cazzie and the millions of other black neighbors who need our support.

The racial revolution in American life has made us see the need for deep social and economic change. The black has held up a mirror to American life and one of the

30

many evils reflected in the mirror is the truth that, in an age of great prosperity, one out of every five Americans live in poverty, below the level of human dignity. We now know that civil rights laws, which protect legal rights — vital as they are — do not touch the deeper problems of the black. What good is the right to eat in a non-segregated restaurant if you don't have the money to eat there? What is the good of a non-discriminatory hotel if you don't have a job which makes it possible to afford to go to a hotel? The lessons of the Black Revolution make it clear that jobs, housing, and education must be made available to every American. Government at all levels has begun to play a major role in the war on poverty. Poverty had long existed in American life, obviously. But as the black finally compelled the white man to really *see* him — as the black, in short, became visible in America — so the poor (white and black) became truly visible for the first time in American history.

The American war on poverty is a challenge to every conscience, for poverty reflects our failure to live up to our religious and democratic ideals. Mankind's first war on poverty was set up in the Bible and, in a sense, Judaism has battled poverty through all of Jewish history. In the Jewish value system all wealth comes from God. Since wealth stems from God, it must be used to advance God's purpose. The idea of the "survival of the fittest" goes against the Jewish view. All human life is sacred — the life of the poor man as well as that of the wealthy. Biblical ethics are filled with rules protecting the dignity of the poor. For example, our sages taught: "If two parties come to a court, one clothed in rags and the other in a very expensive garment, the judges should say to the latter: 'Either dress like him or dress the poor man like yourself'" (Shabuoth 31a). What does this mean? When a field was to be harvested, the corners were left uncut; the gleanings of orchard and vineyard were not to be gathered. What remained was for the poor, the stranger, the fatherless, and the widow. These and other restrictions upon the unlimited pursuit of private economic gain grew out of Judaism's claim that human rights must come before property rights.

Justice, not charity, is the total society's debt to the poor. What is the difference between charity and justice? Overcoming poverty is a mitzvah, a divine commandment, a moral duty required by God. But tackling poverty is too big a task to be left to individual action or private charity; it is viewed in Jewish tradition as the job of the whole Jewish community. A vast system of public welfare — the first in history — came about in the talmudic period. By the Middle Ages, communal responsibility covered almost every aspect of life. Market prices were adjusted so that the poor could buy food at cost; wayfarers were issued tickets for free meals and lodgings at homes of members of the community; various societies arranged for free medical care, for visiting the sick, burying the dead, supplying maternity needs and countless other tasks.

The values of the Jewish tradition helped to shape the excellent network of Jewish welfare agencies we have in the United States. It is interesting to note that Jewish welfare funds in the United States appeared decades earlier than — and helped to start — the development of Community Chests and Red Feather agencies in communities. Do you know what the Community Chest is? Find out in your own community. Do you know about the Jewish welfare fund in your town? Would you like to visit the agency?

Perhaps the most important element in the traditional

Jewish attitude toward the poor is that the poor are not blamed — or shamed — for being poor. In Jewish tradition, the poor are not poor because of something wrong in their character or mind or energy. They are poor because of something wrong in the society at large.

Here, Judaism has much to teach the American people. Recently the Gallup Poll found that 54 per cent of the American people believed that a person is poor because of "lack of effort on his own part" rather than due to "circumstances beyond his control." The idea that poverty is the result of laziness and moral inferiority is one of the major barriers to our war on poverty. This idea, derived from the Puritans, originally produced the English Poor Laws, which were later passed on to the American Colonies. Under these cruel laws, the Colonies sought to send the poor — and, therefore, the morally objectionable — back to Europe. The state of Pennsylvania in those days required paupers to wear a badge with the letter "p" on their arm. In many states, beggars were publicly whipped. While such meanness is now a thing of the past, the spirit behind these practices was revealed in the Gallup Poll mentioned above. If poverty will always be with us, and if it comes from man's laziness and failure, why should the total society do anything to get rid of poverty? Making the American public aware of the need for social justice will mean reeducation away from individual selfishness and toward a society which meets the human and social needs of its own citizens. It is important to realize that America has the means to get rid of slums, poverty, and hunger. Much poorer countries have almost achieved these goals already. America will have to decide on its priorities — what comes first — and begin to turn our vast resources to solving the terrible problems of in-

33

justice which shame Americans within our own land.

In addition to equal rights as between black and white, Christian and Jew, rich and poor, we are becoming increasingly concerned with equal rights as between men and women. There is no question that women have gotten an unfair shake and that they are denied equal pay for equal work. Also, there is sexist prejudice in the hearts of many people who think of women only as mothers and housekeepers and not as human beings with equal potential as doctors, lawyers, teachers, legislators, and in any other walk of life. Even our books and movies tend to show females as sex objects rather than equal human beings.

Judaism was not always free of such sexist taint either, and in many ways it still is not. Orthodox Jews separate men from women in religious services. An ancient prayer actually has men giving thanks to God for not being women.

In Reform Judaism, we have insisted on equal rights. Women and men pray together. Women serve as presidents and leaders of congregations. Moreover, we now have several women rabbis and many more are being trained in the seminary. Do you think your congregation would accept a woman rabbi? There are few causes as vital as the cause of insuring full human rights for women through the Equal Rights Amendment and in all other ways in American life and in Jewish life specifically.

Projects

1. In April, 1969, a very famous British writer and scientist named C.P. Snow made a speech in New York City. In that speech he said that Jews are a superior people. He mentioned that such a small number of people had produced about a third of the Nobel Prize winners in the world. The

only way he could explain this, he said, was that there must be something in the Jewish genes which makes them brighter and quicker than others. What do you think of his statement? Do you agree or not? Why? Do you think it is dangerous to think in terms of superior and inferior races? Isn't that what we object to in the idea of white supremacy or Hitler's master race theories? If the answer to Jewish contributions to the world (as in Nobel Prizes) is not to be found in our genes, where then? Our history? Our religion?

2. Do you think there is something in human nature that makes people dislike people who are different? In 1969, an all-white suburban junior high school in Potomac, Maryland, performed an experiment which had unforeseen results. The experiment was intended to help the students understand discrimination (being against somebody just because of his race or religion). Blondes and brunettes were given certain instructions. On one day, the blondes were to use different rest rooms, staircases, water fountains, library tables, etc. They were also told that they were to receive anti-blonde cracks and teasing from the brunettes. Believe it or not, the experiment had to be called off after two days because students (and their parents) felt that it was "getting not quite so funny as it was the first day." Do you think these youngsters got some insight into how it must feel for a black child who is discriminated against? Or a Jewish child in an unfriendly neighborhood?

Another experiment along these lines was carried out in Riceville, Iowa, in the third-grade class of an all-white rural school. Brown-eyed students were given privileges on Friday, their "Discrimination Day," and blue-eyed students on Monday. Although everybody knew they were just acting out a lesson, the "inferior" students began to show strong signs of real anger and frustration. Of course, the "superior" students loved their privileges. A blue-eyed "inferior" student complained, "I felt left out. I felt like slapping a brown-eyed person." Another blue-eyed person said, "I didn't want to work. I didn't feel I was very big." Said another child, "On Monday I was happy because we discriminated against the brown-eyed people. I felt smarter and gooder and meaner than the brown-eyed people."

What do you think was learned by these experiments?

3. One of the major complaints about education in America is that black people are practically invisible in our history and other texts. Some history books even talk about how

pleasant slavery was. Few textbooks really deal with the significant role the black has played in American history. We are not getting a full picture of America. The black child's image of himself is as hurt as yours would be if your history book were written (as some are) from the standpoint of a white Christian America. White people need to know more about blacks, the part they played in the development of America. For example, did you know that a black man was the first American to die in the American Revolution? That a black man performed the first successful open-heart surgery in the world? That a black woman led 300 slaves to freedom on the Underground Railroad? That one of Abraham Lincoln's advisers was a black writer? That a black man discovered how to separate out blood plasma? Don't feel bad if you don't know their names — but see if you can look them up. Look through your history books. See how blacks are treated, if they are at all.

If you can't find out who these people are, write to Foundation for Change, 1841 Broadway, Room 300, New York, N.Y. 10023.

4. There are many thousand black Jews in America. Most of them live in New York City. What do you think it is like to be black and Jewish? For information on their life and problems ask your rabbi and the director of the local Jewish Community Council.

5. Everybody talks about how integration would help the blacks. But how would it help white people?

6. Do a report on the problem of the American Indians. Write to the National Congress of American Indians, 1346 Commonwealth Avenue, N.W., Washington, D.C. 20036; American Indian Information Center, 20-53 19 Street, Astoria, N.Y. 11105; Indian Rights Association, 1505 Race Street, Philadelphia, Pa. 19102.

7. In 1968 there was a big protest about an anti-Jewish poem written by a black girl in New York in the *Westerner Observer*. But most black people do not hate Jews. Do you know who Cheney, Schwerner, and Goodman were? Find out! What can be done to prevent black anti-Semitism and Jewish racism?

8. Arrange to have a meeting with a class of black students from a nearby church.

9. Find out the difference between an integrationist and a separatist. If you were a black child, which side would you be on? Why?

10. What are the main problems facing black people in your community?

11. Socio-Dramas to act out:

(a) Your family is planning to move and you are trying to sell the house. A black couple comes to look at the house and makes an offer. When they leave, your Dad says, "I'd like to do it, but don't we have to ask our neighbors first? After all, *they* will have to live with them, not us." Your mother says, "But that's not fair! Would we check with them if it were a white family?" You are listening. What do you say? What do your parents answer?

(b) You are a black child and your parents are considering buying a home in an all-white neighborhood. Your father says, "Somebody has to be first; why not us?" Your mother says, "No! I don't want us to be guinea pigs. Let somebody else be a pioneer. I don't want my children to have to go through that." What do you say? What did your parents mean? Pick three people in class to play the roles of Mom, Dad, and child.

(c) You get into an argument with a black boy in your school. He hits you and says: "You honky whites are no good!" What do you say? What do you do?

(d) A black child has just transferred into your class. He doesn't know anybody. What do you do? Act it out.

12. Debate:

A black man named James Forman once threatened to interrupt services in churches and temples unless the religious groups pay a half-billion dollars in "reparations" for the injustice that America has done to blacks. What would you say if you were the rabbi and Forman came to your temple?

(a) Read the debate on Jews and civil rights in *Jewish Values and Social Crisis* by Albert Vorspan (New York: Union of American Hebrew Congregations, 1968), on page 53, and debate it in class.

(b) "Blacks Should Be Given a State to Make a Black Republic Within the U.S."

13. Read some of the following:

(a) *The Jackie Robinson Story*, by A. Mann (New York: Grosset & Dunlap).

(b) *A Look Down the Lonesome Road*, by Ralph Creger (New York: Doubleday, 1964).

(c) *Giants of Justice*, by Albert Vorspan (New York: Union of American Hebrew Congregations, 1960).

14. Films to see and show:

(a) *Jackie Robinson Story.*

(b) *Guess Who's Coming to Dinner.*

(c) *Raisin in the Sun.*

The following films can be obtained at Contemporary Films—McGraw-Hill, 1221 Ave. of the Americas, New York, N.Y. 10020:

(d) *Willie Catches On.* A National Film Board of Canada Production. A frank and searching attempt to answer the question of where the seeds of prejudice are implanted.

(e) *Brotherhood of Man.* Produced by UPA for United Automobile Workers. Through animated color cartoons and music, this film treats the problems involved in developing one world. Based on the Public Affairs pamphlet, "Races of Mankind," it stresses the equality of all peoples and their need for brotherhood, if the future of civilization is to be made secure.

(f) *Fable for Friendship.* An animated humorous short portraying the aims and ideals of UNESCO, it deals with the self-imposed "walls" that separate nations and people from each other — walls of prejudice, ignorance, and self-interest.

(g) *The House on Cedar Hill.* A stirring film biography of Frederick Douglas (1817-1895), a black writer, orator, statesman, and leader in the struggle to help his people emerge from slavery. An exciting musical score based upon black folk songs and a narration drawn from his own writings highlight this film that penetrates one of the little-known areas of our history.

(h) *The Quiet One.* Acclaimed as a film classic, it is an unforgettable drama about an unloved child lost in loneliness who drifts into delinquency.

(i) *A Chance for Change.* Preschool-age youngsters in a Headstart center in a poor black community in Mississippi learned not to be afraid of adults, to voice their thoughts and opinions, to make up their own minds, and to begin to work out their own ideas.

(j) *Vision Quest.* A fourteen-year-old Indian boy's life in the mountains and prairies of western Montana.

(k) *I Wonder Why.* A young black girl wonders why "some people don't like me." A narrator expresses the girl's love for the common elements of life as an accompaniment to a series of images representing nature, people, games, religion.

3. Being True to Myself: Personal Relations

A person can grow mentally throughout his life. He can gain more information and facts at any age. But much of the character of a person is formed in childhood. There are people who say that the outline of a person's character is formed by the time he is six; others put it a few years later. This is why a psychiatrist probes an adult patient's childhood memories. But, wherever one puts it, a person who learns in childhood to deceive himself, to lie to others, to hurt other people, and to go along with anything his friends do — that child will probably be that kind of adult. The most important decisions a young person must make are the ordinary ones he faces daily. How he makes those little decisions will shape his character and personality. They will determine the kind of person he will be and the way he will get along with other persons throughout his life. They will decide the kind of values he will live by. For example:

Pete wasn't one of your best friends, but you were classmates in public school, often got invited to the same parties and liked each other pretty well. You regarded Pete as somewhat of a show-off, especially when girls were around, but he was fun. In fact, it was Pete's showing off which caused the problem.

It was a Friday afternoon, and you, Pete, and Janice were walking home from school together. Pete had a slight crush on Janice and he always acted kooky to make her laugh. On that day he acted nuttier than usual. He darted into the street and pretended to direct traffic until he got chased away. Then he climbed to the top of a parked car and did a wild jig up there. Janice laughed and that just seemed to encourage him. You told him to stop it and you told Janice to act her age. She just laughed at you and called you a "drag."

Then Pete climbed down and said: "Think that's something? Watch this! I'm going into Valenti's store to get us something to eat. You stay out here!"

Even Janice seemed nervous as you waited outside. You were plainly scared. In a few minutes, Pete came racing out of the store, thrusting a box of candy in your arms and shouting, "They saw me! Come on, run!" Pete took off like a jack rabbit, Janice racing after him. You froze, just standing there with the box of candy, feeling alone and frightened and confused.

If this were a real situation, what would you do? Force yourself to run away? Throw the candy in a trash basket? Go back into the store and give the stolen item back? If so, would you tell who took it? Or pretend you didn't know the boy's name? When you get home, will you tell your mother what happened? What will you say to Pete and Janice?

Act out the following scenes:

(1) You are standing in front of the store with the box of candy. What will you do? (2) Pretend you decided to go into the store and return the candy. Pick a boy in the class to play the part of Mr. Valenti, the owner. What does each of you say? (3) Imagine you have now gone home. Have a girl in the class play the part of your mother. She asks you what is wrong, you look funny. What do you say? (4) Have a boy play the part of Pete. You go home and call him on the phone. What do you say? What does he?

There are many important principles which are tested in this small story. One, of course, is honesty. Is stealing any less bad if the item is small, like a box of candy? Is stealing less wrong if it's done for a joke? Another principle is truth. Is it all right to lie, or to hold back the truth, to protect a friend?

In Jewish teaching, there is a saying, "Thou shalt not go after a multitude to do evil." This means that you must not do something wrong even if everybody around you is doing it. This is particularly difficult for young people. They like to be popular with their peers (friends and classmates). They hate to be thought finks or tattletales. They often prefer the approval of their own age-group to living up to the teachings of their parents. They often lack the courage to stand up against their own friends. They like to get along by going along.

The pressures on young people today are very strong. Young people are growing up faster than was the case in earlier generations. As a result of these pressures, many young persons are defying the teachings of their parents and the conventions of society. Some early teenagers are taking up cigarettes. Some are even experimenting with drugs. In both cases, the boy or girl has the support of some other youngsters. But, in both cases, he is risking his health and his future. Marijuana is not just a lark. It is a violation of the law. And it can lead to emotional and physical harm and, in some cases, to even more dangerous drugs. Anyone who is weak enough to play around with such dangerous things is playing Russian roulette with his life.

But what about cigarettes? No adult wants you to smoke, but an awful lot of them do. And how many adults do you know who say they want to stop or who have tried and cannot. Why are adults concerned about smoking, yours as well as theirs? The scientific evidence is now clearcut that cigarettes cause serious medical

41

damage. Studies prove that heavy cigarette smoking often leads to lung cancer and heart disease. And experimenting with such things as a pre-teenager can result in habits which can wreck your future. And for what?

Studies show that there are about 300 thousand deaths a year connected with cigarette smoking. A study by Dr. E. Cuyler Hammond of the American Cancer Society proved that a person who smokes two packs or more a day at age twenty-five or thirty-five can expect to live 8.3 years less than a nonsmoker at the same age. Even men smoking fewer than ten cigarettes a day have a life expectancy 2.8 to 4.6 years shorter than nonsmokers. This is why the law forces cigarette companies to state on the package that smoking can be dangerous to health. It not only *can* be. It is. Until such time as cigarettes are banned as a menace to health, each person — especially a young person not yet addicted to the habit — must make his own choice to protect his health and safety.

But, for youngsters, it is especially important to be true to themselves. A person must be more than a carbon copy of his friends and classmates. He must develop an inner radar based on his own conscience and standards and not just be swept along by the emotion of the moment or the pull of others. Sticking up for your own beliefs is the sign of character. It is much more important than the instant popularity of always going along with others. A person must be an individual before he can be true to anybody else. You cannot love or respect anybody else until you respect yourself.

The idea of not "following after a multitude to do evil" is vital for adults, too. In the southern United States, thousands of white people have known in their own hearts that discrimination against blacks is wrong. But many of them also know that it has been that way for centuries and that their own friends are against equal rights for blacks. Sometimes violent organizations, like the Ku Klux Klan, control the community, making it dangerous to speak out for blacks. Therefore, many good people, whose hearts are in the right place, stay silent. The silence of "good people" leaves the field to the bad people — the haters, the bullies, the segregationists. It is unethical to act against another human being because of his color. It is also unethical to stand by and do nothing when others do any evil work. Judaism despises those who "stand by the blood of their brothers."

Can you give an example of somebody who stood up against public opinion to do what was right?

One such person in America is a leader named Ralph Nader. He made a study of automobile accidents a few years ago and discovered that more people are slaughtered on the highways each year than in all our wars put together. Nader found that one of the biggest factors causing these accidents was that the automobile companies were more concerned with speed, power, size, and flashy chrome than with safety. He showed that many automobile deaths could have been prevented by the safer design of cars. He started a national crusade to compel automobile manufacturers to put in safety belts, to put padding on the dashboards, to install a new steering wheel which wouldn't shatter on impact, and to put in many other features to reduce casualties. The automobile companies came back with a fierce campaign to put Nader down. They had detectives spy on him to try to get something on him to force him to drop the campaign! But he refused to stop. In the end, he even moved the Congress to adopt safety standards, which the automobile manufacturers had to apply to every new car. The manufacturers fought to the very end, because the new safety features would add to their costs, but the young man (only twenty-nine at the time) got public opinion behind him — and he won.

Individuals like Nader, Martin Luther King, Jr., or Jackie Robinson had to face hate, threats, abuse, and sometimes violence to change things for the better. But, like the prophets of the Bible, they were guided by what they believe is right.

Rumor

We all seem to get some kind of wicked thrill out of passing along a mischievous tale about somebody else. For example:

Your telephone rings right after dinner. It is your friend, Don, and he's excited. "Hey, did you hear what happened?" he shouts. "Terry's father was arrested for drunk driving." "Really?" you say. "How do you know?" Don tells you that Janie had called to tell him about it. Now what do you do? Do you run in and tell it to your family? Do you stay on the telephone and pass the story on to all your other friends? What do you say to Don? Do you call Terry and ask her if it is true? What *do* you do?

Rumor can become a serious problem for a city or even a whole country. Here is an advertisement published in Detroit newspapers to.stop rumors of racial violence:

Yes, Virginia,
You Are a
Rumormonger
And you're part of quite a grapevine.

44

There are a lot of well-meaning blabbermouths around these days. And they all have their own juicy stories about how hot things are going to be this summer.

What's the harm in stretching the truth a little among friends? Well, Virginia, it's this way.

A few of your emotional friends went right out after your last party and bought guns. They don't know how to use them. But they're armed.

Canned fruit juice will be a little harder to find at the corner grocery. It's all in Mrs. Miller's basement.

Little Johnny Henry's mother won't let him play outside any more.

And several of your neighbors no longer trust the local authorities to handle crises.

Not a bad record, Virginia. Not bad at all for somebody who doesn't know a thing about the situation.

But how about doing everyone a favor? The next time you feel the urge to "spread the word," why don't you go back to gossiping about Millie Tillson's size 46 girdle?

MUST
Men United for Sane Thought

Detroit — and every other city in the United States — has learned that rumors are almost as dangerous as bullets. Rumors have triggered many of our race riots. Some irresponsible person starts a rumor that the police have killed a black, or that blacks have killed a white girl in a park, or that somebody has planned a race rumble for tonight. The rumor spreads like wildfire in an already tense situation. The rumor is like the lighted match dropped into a tinderbox. And the result is disaster.

America has had much bad experience with rumormongering and talebearing. In the 1950's, a senator named Joseph McCarthy caused terrible fear and suspicion throughout America by spreading half-baked rumors that certain high officials were "communists" or "spies" or "traitors." He had no proof for these charges, but by going up and down the country repeating them he succeeded for a while in frightening the whole country and he gained great power. He also destroyed the reputations and lives of many innocent people.

Hitler gained power in Germany by the use of the "big lie," too; in his case, that "Communist Jews controlled Germany." So rumors and gossip can be more than harmless white lies. They can be dangerous weapons. They can help lead to concentration camps and to wars.

Do you think you have ever caused hurt to someone by spreading a false report, passing on a rumor or gossiping about someone? Be honest with yourself. If you passed on an untrue report that, say, a friend's parents are divorcing, or that one of your teachers has a secret and serious ailment, or that one of your classmates smokes in the bathroom, you may touch off a whispering campaign which could cause real mischief. Did you ever play "Telephone"? Or take part in a Rumor Clinic? Then you know how a rumor changes and grows as it passes from mouth to mouth until, finally, it is completely different and much worse than the small and seemingly innocent tale which started it on its flight.

Gossip

Our Jewish ancestors realized what a serious sin talebearing is. They regarded it as a form of bloodless murder, destroying a person's reputation. "Thou shalt not go up and down the land as a talebearer," it is written. It is interesting that this idea was considered important enough to be included in the Ten Commandments. Which commandment are we talking about? Which deals with this idea? Of course it is: "Thou shalt not bear false witness."

In the same spirit, the Talmud teaches: "Be more careful of your neighbor's honor than of your own."

In ancient Jewish courts, no person could be convicted unless two persons were eyewitnesses to the crime. This rule was to prevent anyone from falsely condemning another person. In Jewish tradition, a person's right to privacy and dignity had to be fully protected. Houses had to be built a certain distance from each other and in such a way that nobody could spy on his neighbors. Jewish law condemned anyone who broke a confidence, or testified falsely, or failed to rebuke a gossipmonger.

In modern times, the Jewish community has been true to these ancient teachings by fighting against politicians like Joseph McCarthy and various groups who hurt people unfairly by loose charges and character assassination.

Gossip is a form of stealing. To amuse yourself and your friends, you are stealing the honor and dignity of another person. "Do not do unto others as you would not have them do unto you" means, at the very least, do not steal from him — either his property or his reputation.

Gossiping, stealing, and lying are obvious ways you can hurt other people and, in doing so, yourself as well. But, there are also more subtle ways to treat people with disrespect. How do you relate to somebody who is different, especially somebody who is handicapped in some way. For example:

Hank lives near you. He is a very pleasant, nice-looking boy but he has a difficult problem of stuttering. He stutters badly when he is under tension. One day you and a bunch of your friends, including Hank, are playing a game in the school playground. One of the kids tells a joke about how a stutterer goes to a radio station to audition for the job of announcer. When he is turned down for the job, he is asked why he didn't get it. He answers: "Be-Be-Be-cause they're a b-b-b-bunch of ant-ant-anti-Semites." Everybody laughs. The joker points to Hank, who is red-faced, and yells: "Hey, Hank, why don't you become a radio announcer?" Do you join in the laughter? Do you try to stop the joker and the other kids? Do you try to understand what Hank is feeling? Or do you just go along quietly?

There are some youngsters who are so weak inside of themselves that they have to build themselves up by tearing others down. This is also one explanation for bigots. As you know, youngsters can be very cruel. Their cruelty is increased when others let them get away with bullying people. Have you heard of the book *Lord of the Flies?* Could children be *that* cruel? The worst bullies are not always those who beat up people with their fists. The worst bullies are those who pick at somebody's weakness in order to get laughs or attention at that person's expense. Can you give an example? How should we deal with such youngsters?

It is easy to get along with other children who are just like us. One of the troubles with most of the neighborhoods in which we live is that we tend to live with people who are just like us — the same race, economic condition, and sometimes even the same religion as ourselves. Many Jewish people live in largely Jewish neighborhoods, just as blacks, Irish, Italians, and others tend to live in their own neighborhoods. For blacks, this kind of segregation is forced upon them by discrimination. For others, it is usually self-segregation by choice. Do you understand the difference? Is self-segregation a good thing or a bad thing?

One result of living in self-segregated neighborhoods is that we often do not learn to live with people of other races and backgrounds. We do not learn to enjoy differences. We sometimes develop false feelings that we are

48

better than others. We tend to be rather frightened of people from other racial backgrounds. And the problem is even worse because, once we get to college, we must learn how to live comfortably with people from all backgrounds. And the world itself is shrinking because of modern jets and telstar T.V. Remember, most of the people in the world do not look like us. Most of the world is not white, not Christian, not Jewish, and not American. To be a full citizen of such a world we will have to know how to appreciate and enjoy the differences among all groups of people. When we are not prepared in our early years to get along easily with blacks and Chinese and poor people and Italians and Puerto Ricans and other groups, we may experience a shock when we leave the false security of our own home and neighborhood. We cannot live in a ghetto all our lives, and most of us do not want to. We must live in the real world with all its risks, conflicts, and exciting experiences of human contacts.

It is very important to our own mental health for us to get to know and appreciate people from all backgrounds. We should learn to play together and work together on common projects. We should understand something of the religion of our neighbors as well as the cultures of other nationality groups. Does this mean that we should date non-Jewish kids? Does it mean that intermarriage is a necessary and good thing? How do you think your parents would feel about interfaith dating? Why do you think it is that Jewish parents are usually so uptight when their children date non-Jews? Write your answers to these questions on one side of a sheet of paper. Get your parents to write *their* answers to the same questions on the other side. Compare the difference of opinion.

It is important to understand why Jewish parents are

so upset about interfaith dating. Why do you think it is? Right. Obviously they fear that such dating might become serious and lead later to interfaith marriage. There is no doubt that some parents get much too nervous and go to silly lengths to prevent social contacts between their children and non-Jewish children before the youngsters are even in their teens. But their fear of interdating is not altogether silly, and it's important to understand. The Jewish people is a small group. There are only fourteen million Jews in the world, only five million in the United States. Hitler killed six million Jews — one out of every three Jews in the world. Jews tend, for many reasons, to have smaller families than do non-Jews. Each year, a higher number of American Jews marry out of the faith. Sometimes their partners convert to Judaism; usually they do not. Most of the time, the children of such intermarriages are not raised as Jews. The Jewish people, who kept their faith and their spirit throughout all the centuries of persecution and poverty, would not survive very much longer if the trend toward intermarriage gets much stronger. Is that something worth worrying about or not?

Of course, a young Jewish person who falls in love with someone who doesn't happen to be Jewish doesn't think much about these things. He or she thinks only of individual happiness. But does the young person also have a duty to think about the future of the Jewish people? What do you think?

Even if the young person says baloney, I couldn't care less about what my marriage will do to the survival of the Jews, there is also the fact that an interreligious marriage is less likely to be a happy one. Marriage is a very difficult undertaking, at best. In America, almost one out of every three marriages ends in divorce. The best marriages are those between two persons who share common backgrounds and interests. When the husband and wife come from different religious backgrounds, this adds just one more possible tension to the marriage. Sometimes, the husband and wife tell each other that religion means very little in their lives anyway, so what difference does it make? When children come, however, the differences can no longer be shoved under the rug. How are the children to be raised? What church or synagogue should they go to? What religious education, if any, should they get? How will the youngsters know just *who* and *what* they are? Many marriages have run aground on just these rocky questions.

It is natural that most Jewish youngsters regard the attitudes of their parents as old-fashioned. And it is true there is something weird about those Jewish parents who are Jewish in name only and have nothing to do with a synagogue or anything else Jewish, but who hit the panic button when their child goes off and marries out of the faith. Yet it is not fair to say, as many young people do, that Jewish parents are against intermarriage because they really think Jews are better than other people or that they are prejudiced against other religions and races.

The Jewish opposition to intermarriage is very clear in the Bible. This opposition has nothing to do with race or color. Moses married Zipporah, a dark-skinned woman. The most touching story of interreligious marriage is the Book of Ruth. Read it. As you see, Ruth married a son of Naomi. When he died, Ruth was told by Naomi that she should feel free to return to her own people. But Ruth replied, in words that have become legendary: " ... Whither thou goest, I will go ... thy people shall be my people. ..." In effect, Ruth converted to Judaism and chose to cleave to the Jewish faith. Thousands of non-Jews, mostly those who marry Jews, have converted to the Jewish faith. Some are famous, including the late Marilyn Monroe, Elizabeth Taylor, and Sammy Davis, Jr. Judaism is not a closed shop. Anyone who seriously and freely wishes to join, and is willing to follow the course of study leading to conversion, is welcome.

While Jews will accept converts, Jews do not have missionaries who go out and seek converts. There are some rabbis and other Jewish leaders who believe that we should go out actively to seek converts. Have you ever heard of Billy Graham, the famous Christian evangelist? Do you think Jews should have giant rallies, distribute literature, talk to people, set up special centers in our various cities to help persuade Gentiles to come to Judaism? One of the arguments in favor of this is that it would make up for the loss of people through inter-marriage. Another argument is that often the newly converted are the most enthusiastic Jews. Among the arguments against this idea are these: Jews have always resented Christians trying to convert them, so why should we practice what we have preached against? Also, when you try to convert somebody to your religion, there is a slight suggestion of superiority on your part. And, also, there are so many Jews who neither know nor care about Judaism, why don't we "convert" them before we spread ourselves so thin? What do you think of these arguments? Arrange a debate: "Resolved: Jews in America Should Start an Active Missionary Campaign to Convert Non-Jews to Judaism."

There is another problem connected with this that causes much argument — whether or not a rabbi should be willing to officiate at an interfaith marriage. Pretend, for example, that your older brother or sister decides to marry a non-Jew. Pretend, furthermore, that your parents come finally to accept the idea. They go to the rabbi and ask him to conduct the ceremony. Chances are the rabbi will ask; Does the non-Jewish partner intend to convert? If the answer is yes, the rabbi will no doubt be willing to officiate. If the answer is no, the rabbi may refuse. Some people are very angry at this policy of rabbis and they say it is unfair and even bigoted. But, if you remember what we said earlier in this chapter, you will at least understand the rabbi's position. Why not invite the rabbi to class and discuss this situation with him? Do you agree with the rabbi's position on this or do you think it is wrong? Why?

Projects

1. Debate: "Jews Should Start a Missionary Program."
2. Debate: "Jews Should Continue to Oppose Inter-marriage.
3. Discuss: Rabbi Joachim Prinz was a rabbi in Berlin when Hitler came to power. Speaking at the March on Washington, Rabbi Prinz said: "When I was the rabbi of the Jewish Community in Berlin under the Hitler regime, I learned many things. The most important thing that I learned in my life and under those tragic circumstances is that bigotry and hatred are not the most urgent problem. The most urgent, the most disgraceful, the most shameful, and the most tragic problem is *silence.*" What did he mean? Do you agree?
4. Discuss: Should the synagogue religious school teach the evils of cigarette smoking or is that purely an individual matter?
5. Discuss: Should the manufacture of cigarettes be made illegal?
6. Making a Code of Decency:
Here is a code of behavior written by a young Jewish boy. See if you can improve upon it. What do you agree with? What

53

do you disagree with? How would you change it? Do we need a code at all? Why do you think he wrote one?

First Commandment: I am an important person — to me the most important person. But I know that I am not the only person in the world. Every other human being also needs attention, and only God is the center of the universe.

Second Commandment: I shall not make a god of group approval; rather, I shall maintain my individual integrity.

Third Commandment: I shall not become vain and place such things as physical beauty and popularity above more important standards of individual worth.

Fourth Commandment: I shall remember that education is the privilege of free men, and that it is my responsibility to make the most of this opportunity as my contribution to strengthening democracy.

Fifth Commandment: I shall respect my father and my mother and share with them my problems and my desire for guidance in making my decisions.

Sixth Commandment: I shall not tell "white lies"; they are only crutches and are an easy way to avoid the reality of truth.

Seventh Commandment: I shall not tell or listen to "off-color" stories; boy-girl relationships should be kept on a high level.

Eighth Commandment: I shall not cheat others by giving or receiving information on examinations; I shall not cheat myself by accepting minimum requirements as a maximum goal.

Ninth Commandment: I shall not tear down another's character through gossip; nor judge my fellow man on the basis of racial, national, or religious heritage; but on his individual worth.

Tenth Commandment: I shall not envy; each of us has so many blessings that we should count our own, instead of wishing for material possessions of others.

Based on the preparation, the class may develop a decalogue for itself out of its discussion.

7. The Problem of The Four Grandchildren:

Imagine that Jack Mishnick, the richest man in the Jewish community, just died. He left much of his money to good causes, both Jewish and general. But there was a very peculiar item in his will. It said: "Now that I have provided for my family and for the causes in which I believe so deeply, I set aside the sum of $10,000 to go to each of my four grandchildren, and an extra $20,000 to go to whichever one of the four is deemed most likely to grow up to become a *Good Jew.* This extra $20,000 is not to be divided up among the four of them. I want the group which makes the decision as to which child should get it to interview each of my grandchildren, ask whatever questions they want about the family and home each comes from, and make an honest and binding decision."

That was all the will said. To help us make the decision in this strange matter, we have gotten together some basic facts about each of Mishnick's four grandchildren and their families. Here are the facts:

Scott is eleven years old. He is an only child. His parents are quite comfortable. The family lives in a nice, large, old home in the suburbs. Scott's parents are not religious but they belong to the synagogue. They do not go to services often — mainly the High Holy Days. Scott does not go often either. Scott does not like to go to religious school but he usually does go, partly because of the strong influence his grandparents had on him, partly because his parents say "we joined the synagogue so you could learn what it is to be Jewish." Scott is an average student. He is the biggest giver to Keren Ami, never giving less than a dollar.

He is this generous because his father has taught him his belief that the most important quality in a Jew is charity. Scott's father is himself one of the biggest contributors to good causes. Scott is looking forward to his Bar Mitzvah in two years, because his parents have promised him a color television set of his own in honor of that event. Scott receives very good grades in public school, but his grades in religious school are about average. Scott is a very good athlete, especially in basketball, and his ambition is to become a professional basketball player. He reads mostly about sports and comics and his biggest argument with his parents is that they always say he watches too much television.

Beth is twelve years old. Beth looks forward to going to college in Israel. She is even trying to persuade her parents to let her go next year to spend the summer working on a kibbutz. Israel is very precious to Beth's parents and to Beth. Her father is president of the local Zionist organization. During the Six Day War in Israel, her father went to the bank, borrowed $5,000, and contributed it to the United Jewish Appeal to help during the emergency. Beth was proud, but not surprised, because her father had always taught her that a love of the Jewish people, and especially of the Jewish state of Israel, is one of the most important duties of a Jew. Beth's parents do not believe in God; the family does not belong to a synagogue. Sometimes Beth gets unhappy about that, because many of her friends do belong and she feels she is missing something. Her parents say that they teach her more about being Jewish in their home than she would learn in all that "Mickey Mouse stuff they teach at religious school." The most important thing about being Jewish, they say, is to learn Hebrew, which she will do in Israel, and to do all in her power to keep Israel alive and healthy. Beth reads many books about Israel and sometimes she thinks she would like to move there permanently when she is older. Sometimes Beth wishes she had insisted that her parents send her to a religious school and she is especially sad that she is not part of a synagogue youth group.

Peter is eleven. His mother is president of the synagogue sisterhood and his father is a member of its board. Pete's family observes the holidays at home. They light the candles, recite the Kiddush and the Motzi for the Sabbath. Peter complains about Friday evening, because his parents insist he be home for the Sabbath and, usually, the family goes to synagogue together. Pete has gone to the Camp for Living Judaism of the UAHC the past two summers and he loved it. His father and mother regard themselves as religious Jews. Pete's father builds large housing developments and he was recently denounced in the press by a black organization because no black families live in one of his developments. "I have nothing against blacks or any other group," Pete's father told the reporters, "but I know that most of the people who live in my homes do not want to live in a mixed neighborhood. I think it would be wrong for me to force my liberal ideas on them." Pete knows how upset his father was during that time, especially when one of his father's own brothers publicly disagreed with him. Pete wonders if his father is doing right in this matter, but he does not feel it would be his place to say anything.

Ruth is fourteen. Her family is active in the synagogue. Her father is chairman of the social action committee. Her father and Pete's father are brothers and both families had a bitter falling-out over the black situation. At the Passover Seder where the entire family group had joined together as they had every year, Ruth's father had said to Pete's father, "Look, I don't know how you can say the words of the Haggadah about 'let us remember the heart of the stranger, for we were strangers in Egypt'! The strangers in America are the black people, and you are one of the people who keep them out! How can you call yourself a religious man when you treat human beings on the basis of color and not as equals?" Pete's father was furious. "What has religion got to do with business? Would you feel better if I went bankrupt? And why don't you mind your own business?" This argument got nasty and even spilled over to the children. Ruth stopped talking to Pete after that. Ruth's mother became very angry at Ruth. "How dare you blame Peter for what his father does! That is mean and unfair! I don't think your father had any business criticizing Pete's father, but that certainly doesn't involve you!" Ruth agrees with her father that to be Jewish means to work for justice among all men, even if that gets some people — even relatives — angry. But Ruth's mother says that one of the greatest things about Jews is their sense of family — and loyalty to family — and she says Ruth and her father were destroying that quality.

Get four different members of the class to represent each of the four grandchildren. Have each one speak as if he were really Scott, Beth, Pete, or Ruth. Let each explain why he thinks he will be the best Jew. Let the class question each child. Then have the class discuss which child should win. In that discussion, what are the things we should look for in each child to decide which one is the most promising Jew? List the things that you think are important in judging how good a Jew a person is. What are the strengths of each child? What are the weaknesses? Who is the best Jew? Is being a good Jew any different from just being a good person? Remember, this is only a matter of opinion. Is there a *right* answer? It all depends on what *you* think are the most important things about a good Jew. Is it knowledge? Belief in God? Doing good? Synagogue attendance? Charity? Education? Love of Israel? Is it all of these? You decide by a class vote.

4. The Violence of Man

In this generation there have been terrible assassinations of American leaders — John F. Kennedy, Martin Luther King, Jr., and Robert F. Kennedy. There have also been terrible race riots in the cities with hundreds injured and much destruction. There have been disorders and demonstrations where many students have been hurt. What is wrong with America that leads to such dreadful violence? What can be done to cut down on such bloodshed?

Violence has always been a big problem in America. Ever since the white man came to these shores, blood has been freely spilled. First it was Indian blood. Later, blacks were brought here in chains from Africa and kept in slavery by brute force. In pioneer days, almost every American carried a gun and knew how to handle it. Arguments were settled by the barrel of a gun. Life was rugged and it was cheap. Violence was common.

Today guns have become a major problem in this country. Every two minutes a gun is used to kill or wound an American citizen. More than 7,500 people were murdered with firearms in 1968. Since 1900, three-quarters of a million people have died in the United States by guns — through murder, suicide, and accident. This is 200 thousand more than the number of Americans killed in all of our wars.

These statistics of the Justice Department bear out the words of former President Johnson that America has a "record of violent death and destruction that shames our history."

There is no civilized nation in which it is as easy for

the mentally ill, drug addicts, criminals, and minors to buy firearms as in our own. Yet a Gallup Poll in 1967 showed that 85 per cent of all adult Americans were in favor of a law to control guns, including the registration of all guns. But the wishes of the majority for a sensible control of guns have been blocked by the powerful pressures of the National Rifle Association and various gun manufacturers upon our congressmen and senators. How could this happen?

Here are the arguments of those who are against a gun control law:

1. They say that the right "to keep and bear arms," guaranteed in the Second Amendment to the Constitution, would be broken by such legislation.

2. They are afraid that gun control laws would hurt the sportsman who uses guns for hunting and marksmanship.

3. They claim that the legislation would not lower crime rates, as criminals would still be able to get guns illegally.

These arguments are weak. The Second Amendment of the Constitution states: "A well-regulated militia being necessary to the security of a free state, the right of the people to keep and bear arms shall not be infringed." This was written in order to guarantee each state a militia, and the Supreme Court has stated many times that it does not guarantee to individual citizens the right to bear arms. If there is a right to bear arms, it is not as important as the right to life. There is a right to own an automobile, but still the automobile must be registered and anyone who wants to drive it must be licensed.

No one claims that gun control legislation would end all violence and crimes. But the fact is that it does cut down the number of crimes in which guns are involved.

In states with strong firearms laws, the percentage of murders in which guns are used ranges from 30-40 per cent; in states with weak laws the range is from 60-70 per cent, much higher than in the former group. A comparison of our country with other nations is shocking. In countries which require registration and licensing of guns, the rate of gun murders is five to fifty times lower than ours: 2.7 per 100,000 population in the United States as against .52 in Canada, .12 in West Germany, and .05 in Britain.

Estimates of the number of firearms owned by private citizens in the United States range from 50 to 200 million. Each day the papers carry stories of personal tragedy caused by someone who should not have been allowed to own a gun. Political assassinations have threatened the foundations of the American system of government.

The adult organizations of Reform Judaism have called on Congress to adopt strong gun control legislation, including licensing and registration. The members of the National Federation of Temple Youth, the teenage organization of Reform Judaism, have called for a complete ban on all firearms except for the armed forces. They would forbid guns for hunting, and even policemen would be limited to night sticks as they were until recently in England. Do you agree with the youngsters or the adults about how strong a gun control law should be passed? Debate the issue.

We will not be able to stop the crazy traffic in guns until the people demand that their congressmen vote for a tough law that will make every person get a license before he can own a gun. The law should register every gun, so that we can make sure that youngsters, mentally ill people, political extremists, lunatics, and criminals do not have use of them. Many synagogues are circulating petitions to members of their congregations and to others in the community to present their views to their congressmen. A petition is printed at the end of this chapter. Why not organize a petition campaign in your synagogue and town?

Another reason for violence in this country is the fact that millions of Americans live in miserable slums and suffer injustice and racial discrimination (see Chapter 2). Race riots are the most extreme form of violence in the ghetto, but there is also a daily round of muggings, gang fighting, and other outbreaks. People who feel trapped, helpless, and angry and who feel they have no stake in their society explode into violence very easily. How can this be dealt with? By more police and armored cars? By getting rid of the slums, the unjust conditions, and poverty? What would you suggest? What would you do about this if you were President of the United States?

We see so much violence around us that we tend to think that something new and frightening is happening to America. That may be so, but we should remember that violence in the slums existed in America long before black militancy was born. In the decades from 1830 to 1870, Irish immigrants caused riots in almost every major city. Some of the worst riots took place in New York City in the 1863 Draft Riots. At that time, the Irish rebelled not only against the draft (which, in those days, allowed rich men to escape by paying $300 for a substitute) but also against the miserable conditions in which they lived. Irish Americans finally gave up violence when they became policemen, political figures, contractors, and labor leaders. In other words, when they made it into the system, their family life improved,

61

their attitudes changed, and they ceased rebelling. Just as Irish urban violence faded away when the Irish gained a fair share of power and dignity, so black violence will stop when our society gives blacks a fair chance to achieve decent goals within the system.

Some people feel that we have learned to accept violence. They point out that the long war in Vietnam makes us all take human life cheaply. We read about body counts and watch actual battles on television and it dulls our senses. Who is horrified, except the families of the victims? We get used to the statistics of death. A body count is not just a number, it means so many fathers, brothers, sons, and sometimes mothers and sisters. Do you agree with this opinion? Do you think this war so far away has increased violence inside America?

It is also sometimes claimed that the violence on television and in our movies has warped our minds. There are people who say the popularity of fighting and killing on our television screen has built up an appetite for violence in Americans. They say we are left cold if the show doesn't have the clout of a few fights and some blood on the rug. They call for a code to reduce the violence in our television shows and motion pictures. What do you think? Do you think all this television violence affects you, your thinking and feeling? Would we be better off if the government passed a law to keep violence off our television? Could that be done? Or would that be censorship? Would you and other members of the class like to conduct an experiment of checking television programs to see how many of the programs have violence in them? If your study proves that violent action is very common, would you want to write to the television networks to protest? What do you think?

Violence is growing in America. In addition to the

high rate of murder, it is estimated that forty thousand children each year are seriously beaten by their parents or their brothers or sisters. There have been 230 riots in American cities during the past five years. In New York City in 1967 alone, vandals broke 202,712 school windows and 360,000 pay telephones. Damage to the parks amounted to $750,000 in that one year. Scientists studying violence in American life did a test of vandalism in two cities — Palo Alto, California and New York (Bronx). In each city a car was left across the street from a college campus. The cars had raised hoods and were without license plates. Hidden cameras were concealed inside the cars. In Palo Alto — a smaller city — the abandoned car was untouched for more than a week. On the other hand, the car left in the Bronx was attacked twenty-three separate times, usually in daylight, and was soon smashed into "a battered useless hulk of metal." Not only that. The attacks in the Bronx were almost always witnessed by well-dressed, clean-cut persons, often adults, who sometimes stopped to chat amiably with the persons looting the car. The social scientists felt that the sheer bigness of American cities — and the pressures built up in these cities — can stir up the violence in each of us. What do you think? Do you agree with the scientists? What can be done to bring down the pressure?

There is no doubt that violence breeds more violence. What should we do with the violent person? What should be done with the person who commits murder? In most American states, society takes his life. This is called capital punishment or the death penalty. But isn't that only making matters worse by making the state — and, therefore, all the people — *legal* murderers? Shouldn't we try to save the person who has committed crimes, even the bloodiest crimes, instead of killing him? Is it right to repay violence with violence? There is a debate throughout the United States and the world as to whether or not the death penalty should be wiped off the law books. Those who are against the death penalty — or capital punishment — say it is immoral and barbaric and is a form of cruel and unusual punishment. Those who are for it say it is the only way to keep other people from committing new crimes. What do you think?

Another problem in America is what to do with violent persons sentenced for crimes. One answer is to punish them. But punishment does not usually improve a person or make him fit for decent life in a civilized society. One trouble with the prison system in America is that we merely punish people: stick them into grim jails, put them in touch with even more hardened criminals, fail to give them psychological treatment or to train them for a decent job, and then release them into society. Do you know what happens to persons who have been in jail? Three out of four go back to jail sooner or later. They have not been helped or improved — only punished. This makes many of them even more bitter and all they want to do is punish society back. Some thoughtful Americans are trying to think up better ways of dealing with crimes and criminals. One of our biggest prisons, Sing Sing, has just trained a group of prisoners to run computers. When they leave prison, these men will all have good jobs, paying at least $10,000 a year. Is it less likely that they will continue a life of crime? Or do you think that such a program would just be rewarding the criminal for his crime?

But what if somebody takes a life not out of hatred and vengeance, but out of love? Recently, a young boy was arrested and charged with taking the life of his mother.

He had taken a gun from his father's drawer and shot his mother in her sleep. Obviously that boy had committed a terrible crime. He did not deny shooting her. But he explained that his mother was dying of an incurable disease, that she was suffering horribly, that he loved her very much, and that she had begged him to put her out of her misery. He said he could not stand to see her suffer any longer. This is known as a mercy killing (or euthanasia). If you had been a member of the jury which tried this boy, how would you have voted? Should the law be changed so that persons suffering the agony of an incurable disease can be legally put to rest? Or would that be a violation of the commandment: "Thou shalt not murder"? Debate this issue, pro and con. For information on the subject, write Euthanasia Educational Council, Inc., 250 West 57 Street, New York, N.Y. 10019.

One of the reasons for the youth revolt, the hippie movement, and the "flower children" is a plea for love instead of so much violence and brutality. Many of these young people are trying, often in foolish ways, to find a more gentle way of life. The late Robert Kennedy used to speak of the need to tame the savagery of man and make gentle the life of the world. You can sense this disgust with brutality in the songs of Simon and Garfunkle, the Beatles, Donovan, Buckley, and the other popular singers of folk and rock.

Listen to your own records and write down examples of lyrics which try to show up our violent ways and suggest a loving way for human beings to treat each other (for examples, see Chapter 9).

On the other hand, more and more people, especially the young and the black, have come to believe that the only way to improve things in America is by violent demonstrations. They have come to believe that nonviolence does not work. They think that only force will make people sit up and change things for the better. What these young people ignore is the fact that violence feeds on itself and that justice can never be achieved in a disorderly society which comes apart at the seams. What do you think? Can you think of any cases where violence would be proper? How about self-defense? What if a person is starving while others have plenty?

Of course, the most terrible problem of violence is war. Mankind has suffered from wars since the beginning of time. Some people think that this is because of human nature — that we each have inside us a need to fight. Do you agree with that? There are some primitive groups in the South Pacific and elsewhere who settle their arguments without violence; and there are also some countries, like Switzerland, which stay neutral in every war and simply do not fight. So perhaps it is not simply a matter of human nature. There are some people, called pacifists, who believe that it is never right to fight, even if you are attacked. Do you agree? Are wars always wrong? Can you think of a proper reason for a country to go to war? Can you think of an improper reason? Can you give an example?

The problem of the State of Israel is a good example. More than any other religion, Judaism believes in peace. The prophets taught of the great day when nations shall convert their swords into plowshares and make war no more. Yet, the State of Israel has had to fight several wars against its Arab neighbors. What choice did they have when their Arab neighbors sought to destroy them and to drive them into the sea? The Israelis would like nothing better than to sit down with their Arab neighbors and make a peace treaty. But the Arab rulers have not wanted that. They organize terrorists to slip into

Israel and blow up innocent civilians, including women and children. The Israelis appeal to the United Nations. When that does no good, the Israelis feel that they must organize "reprisals" by which their troops go into an Arab country and destroy a refinery, or a base, or an airport. Then the Arab terrorists vow to spread more terror, the Israelis hit back again, and the vicious circle gets wider. What is the solution? Entebbe was a good example. Terrorists hijacked an Air France plane, flew it to Uganda, and threatened to kill 108 innocent people, mostly Israelis. The world sat on its hands. What could Israel do to protect its citizens? It was compelled to use force, flying its commandos to Entebbe to destroy the terrorists, and release the innocents in the greatest act of liberation in our time.

Jewish teaching is strongly opposed to violence. Every human being is seen as a child of God — and as a neighbor. The first teaching of the Jewish religion is to "love your neighbor as yourself." There is a story in the Talmud of a man being attacked by his enemy. Does the person attacked have the right to kill his attacker? No, the Talmud says, "for what makes you think your blood is redder than his?" What do you think the rabbis meant by this story?

God despises human vengeance. "Vengeance is the Lord's," says the Bible, not man's. There is a story that when the children of Israel crossed the Red Sea and saw the Egyptians drowning behind them, they cheered and sang songs of joy. God chided the Hebrews by saying: "My children are dying and you sing songs." What does this story mean?

Our forefathers often fought wars, but they never made heroes out of warriors. Saints and scholars were Jewish heroes. Who are our heroes today? Isn't it athlet-

67

es, television and movie stars? King David was a great man, but he was not allowed to build the Temple because his hands were regarded as bloody because of his military record. Not only was the man who did violence seen as a sinner; so was the man who stood around and did nothing when other people were being hurt. "He who saves one life, it is as if he saves the world," the Talmud says. But—"Neither shalt thou stand idly by the blood of your neighbor" (Lev. 19:16). Can you give examples of people who have lived by these ideals?

Loving one's neighbor is not so hard, after all. Usually our neighbors don't beat us up or bust up our homes. But how are we to treat an enemy? The Book of Proverbs tells us *not* to say: "I will do to him as he has done to me; I will pay the man back for what he has done" (24:29). In other words an eye for an eye is wrong. But what then is a person to do if he is wronged? The Bible says: "If a man returns evil for good, evil will not depart from his house" (Prov. 17:13). What do you think this means? Can you give an example? Once the rabbis discussed the meaning of this teaching as follows: "R. Simeon b. Abba said: 'Not only he who returns evil for good, but even he who returns evil for evil, evil will not depart from his house.'"

What did they mean? Did they mean you have to do good to one who has wronged you? Is that good advice for real people or is it too much to expect of human nature? Why should a person have to go out of his way to help someone who has hurt him? Does this make sense? Why or why not?

The rabbis ask another interesting question. Who should we help first, a friend or an enemy? The answer of the rabbis is, believe it or not, the enemy. Can you imagine what they had in mind? The rabbis felt that the enemy is both a child of God and a neighbor, and you must fight against your natural drive to ignore him or to hurt him. The rabbis felt that love and brotherhood can melt hate. As one rabbi explained, "By seeing that the other man is trying to please him, his heart will change and he will repress [put away] his hatred."

Is the rabbi right? Would it work between the Israelis and the Arabs? Between the United States and the Soviet Union? Could Jews have melted the hatred of the Nazis? Can you think of an example in your own life where this did or did not work? The rabbis of old believed it was very important for every man to try to control his impulse to hate because hate feeds on hate. Even the hate you keep inside yourself is wrong for "You shalt not hate your brother in your heart" (Lev. 19:17).

How can Jewish teaching expect a person to be so good that he can love somebody who does something wrong against him? The answer is that we should hate the *sin* but not the *sinner*. The rabbis tell the following story from the third century C.E.: R. Alexandri said, "Two donkey drivers who were walking by the way hated each other. One of their donkeys sat down. His companion saw it, and passed on. When he had passed, he thought: It is written in the Torah, 'If you see the donkey of one who hates you . . . you shall surely help him to lift it up.' Immediately, he returned and loaded with him. He (the former) began to say to himself: So-and-so is thus my friend and I did not know. Both entered an inn and ate and drank. Who is responsible for their making peace?"

In other words, the man who helped his enemy succeeded in washing away the other man's hate. Isn't that better than letting a feud get bigger and more bitter until each person is poisoned by hate?

All this is well and good for a slight hurt or a misunderstanding, you might say, but what if somebody sets out to kill you? Are you supposed to sit by and let him do it? Isn't that asking us to act like angels and not real persons? Jewish teaching is not so foolish as that. "If a man comes to kill you, rise early and kill him first" (Berakhot 58a). So there is the right to kill in self-defense. But how far does that go? One of the most exciting stories in the Bible is about Jacob and Esau, the two famous brothers who feuded with each other over their father Isaac's birthright. The rabbis discussed this centuries later and wondered why Jacob didn't kill Esau when he had the chance.

"Then Jacob was greatly afraid. Do you think that Jacob really feared Esau, that he could not overcome him? It is not so. Rather, why did he fear him? That he would not stumble into the shedding of blood. Jacob thought, Anyway you want, if I kill him I will transgress [the command] 'Thou shalt not murder.'"

What does this story mean? Doesn't it say that even killing in self-defense might be murder? Do you agree? There is still another famous biblical story. This one is about the famous clash between Saul and David. The mad King Saul, blind with jealousy of the dashing young David, chases him in order to kill him. David hides in a cave. Saul enters the cave, but in the darkness doesn't see David. But David sees Saul. Does he kill him? Should he have?

The Bible recalls: "And Saul went in [the cave]. ... Now David and his men were sitting in the innermost parts of the cave. And the men of David said to him, 'Here is the day of which the Lord said to you, "Behold, I will give your enemy into your hand, and you shall do to him as it shall seem good to you." ' Then David arose and stealthily cut off the skirt of Saul's robe. And afterward David's heart smote him ..." (I Sam. 24:3-5).

70

How do you figure this story? What happened? What did David do? What is meant by the words, his "heart smote him"? Was David a coward? Or was he brave enough to keep from killing the man who wanted to kill him?

One of the rabbinic sages explained it this way: His urge appeared and said, "If you fell into his hand he would have no mercy for you and would kill you. And from the Torah it is permissible to kill him, for he is a pursuer." Accordingly, he [David] leaped and swore twice, "By God, I won't kill him!" (Tanhuma, B'ha'alotkha 10; see Berakhot 62b).

Our ancient teachers went so far as to claim that it is always better to be among the persecuted than among the persecutors, because "there is none among the birds more persecuted than the doves and pigeons, and yet Scripture made them alone among the birds eligible for the altar" (Lev. 1:14). (Now you see why those who are for peace are called "doves.") It is better to suffer than to do violence. The reason for this is that, in Jewish teaching, God is always on the side of the persecuted. But was it really better for six million Jews to suffer and die, or should they have fought the Nazis? Who are the persecuted of today? Are Jews generally on their side? Can we say God is, too?

It would not be easy — and it may be impossible — to live up to such a code of nonviolence. Martin Luther King, Jr., and Mahatma Gandhi did, and they were both killed. If the people of Israel tried to do it, would they be able to survive among Arab powers out to destroy them? Our forefathers could believe in nonviolence and self-suffering because they believed in the mercy of God. David wrote: "Even to a murderer as well as to the slain, to a pursuer as well as to the pursued, I show kindness as to a righteous man." That is what is written: "But as for me, in Thy mercy do I trust; my heart shall rejoice in Thy salvation. I will sing unto the Lord because He has dealt bountifully with me!" (Psalms 13:6). David could say this because he believed in God with absolute confidence. Do we? Can nonviolence work in our lives and in America?

Judaism is even against the violent treatment of animals. Kindness to animals is a mitzvah, and animals can be slaughtered for food only in certain ways that will not cause suffering for the beast. Did you ever hear of a *shochet?* Ask your parents or grandparents, and maybe they will take you to visit a kosher slaughtering house. You will see that animals are slaughtered by a knife stroke which renders them instantly unconscious. This is because the Bible and the Talmud prohibit the abuse of animals.

Earlier in the twentieth century, the genius Albert Einstein once said: "Show me a man who is a hunter and claims to be a Jew, and I will show you a liar." He meant that Jews did not hunt for pleasure. For centuries that was true. In recent decades, some Jews have taken up the sport of hunting. Do you think hunting for pleasure should be permitted? America does not allow bull-fighting. Should we ban hunting, also? Do you think Jews who engage in this sport are breaking Jewish ideals? Debate this. You may wish to invite a father who enjoys hunting to visit with the class so that you can get his point of view.

Of course, Jews are not the only ones who teach about the evil of violence. Jesus once said: "If a man smites you on one cheek, turn the other cheek." And St. Francis of Assisi, a great Catholic saint of the Middle Ages, once recited this beautiful prayer:

Where there is hatred, let me know love.

Where there is injury, pardon.

Where there is doubt, faith.

Where there is despair, hope.

Where there is darkness, light.

But the emphasis in Jewish teaching is especially strong against bloodshed and for peace. "The Torah enjoins us not to run after a mitzvah but to perform it only if it comes to us. With regard to peace, however, it enjoins us to *pursue* it." What does that mean? Do people still hold these beliefs? Can we live with such beliefs in this modern world? Those are the questions we must think through in trying to figure out our own personal code of values to live by.

Projects

1. Debate: "Boxing Should Be Abolished."

2. Debate: "Movies and Television Should Be Censored for Violence."

3. Debate: "Nobody Except the Armed Forces and Police Should Be Permitted to Own Guns."

4. Debate: "Capital Punishment Should Be Abolished."

5. Are the movies too violent? Think of the last three movies you have seen and describe the violent scenes.

6. One of the UAHC camps maintains a rifle range to give young people an opportunity to learn marksmanship. One of the parents protests that the program is a violation of Jewish ideals. There is a meeting of youngsters and adults to decide what to do about it. What do you say? How do you decide?

7. A black boy says that nonviolence doesn't work and that he intends to use force to get his rights. What would you say to him?

8. Write an essay on how mankind can get rid of war.

9. Movies to show:

(a) *War Games.* A full length movie; an ironic commentary on the dehumanization and brutalization of societies by war and by the acceptance of a nuclear world. Actual film of bombings of Dresden, Hamburg, Nagasaki, and Hiroshima. Discuss the meaning of the film. Available from Contemporary Films—McGraw-Hill, 1221 Ave. of the Americas, New York, N.Y. 10020.

(b) *The Magician.* A military officer interests a group of young boys in a deserted shooting gallery. Amusement turns into enjoyment of the powers of destruction. Contact: AFSC/American Friends Service Committee, 15 Rutherford Place, New York, N.Y. 10003 or Sterling Educational Films, 241 East 34 Street, New York, N.Y. 10016.

(c) *Munro* by Jules Feiffer. Satire on what happens when a four-year-old boy gets drafted. Contact: AFSC (above) or Contemporary Films (above).

(d) *Children Adrift.* A study of a lonely boy in a foreign refugee camp outside Paris. An example of the way universal emotions unite human beings of diverse language, nationality, and age. Contact: Contemporary Films (above).

(e) *Albert Schweitzer.* Biography of the Nobel Prize winner, philosopher, theologian, missionary, physician, organist—from birth to his decision at the age of fifty to start his jungle hospital. Contact: Contemporary Films (above).

10. Organize a petition campaign for an effective gun control law. A sample petition follows. You can have this petition mimeographed. Members of the class can gather signatures. Contact other youth groups in synagogues and churches and see if they will help. Call the local newspapers and ask them to write about the campaign. Get your synagogue's Social Action Committee to help. Write a story for the synagogue bulletin. Write to your congressman and your two senators. What else can you do to get the campaign swinging?

11. Organize a class visit to a prison or a juvenile court.

12. Arrange to see the UAHC filmstrip *Call for the Question* which deals with juvenile delinquency and what you and the synagogue can do about it.

Petition

We, the People, citizens, voters and future voters, demand that Congress immediately enact the following legislation:

1. To make it illegal for anyone to purchase hand grenades, bombs, and machine guns.

2. That no person under eighteen be allowed to purchase a lethal weapon.

3. Institute registration procedure for all firearms.

Name   **Address**
1.
2.
3.
4.
5.

Sign your name at the top of the list.

Get four more signatures and mail to the President.

If you really care, make five more copies and mail them to other interested people.

Please mail copies to President Carter, Washington, D.C., to your congressman, and to both your senators.

5. The Struggle of Israel

Israel didn't mean much to you until your older brother, Chuck, went there for a year to study at the Hebrew University. Until then, you were kind of bored with the whole subject. Your parents seemed to talk about it all the time, and they were always so emotional. Sometimes they had tears in their eyes. Your teachers at religious school — they all seemed to say the same things. Besides, the newspapers and television were always talking about Israel — and it seemed always to be about a bombing, or a raid, or a killing. After a while, you kind of turned the whole subject off. But when your older brother decided to enroll at the Hebrew University in Jerusalem for his third year of college, you got a bit more interested. Since Chuck is eight years older than you are, you wondered if he would bother to write you. The truth is that you two didn't talk very much when he was home. He kind of treated you like a nuisance. But — surprise! — he not only wrote you from Israel, he wrote some letters just for you (not family letters), and they were thoughtful and interesting. Seeing Israel through his eyes, catching the contagion of his excitement, made Israel come alive for you.

Dear Debby,

Well, here is your first letter from Your Man in Jerusalem. I'm settled in my little cubicle (room) in the dorm near the University. The room is not much but, wow, what a view! The pink Judean hills stretch outside my window. The flight over here was long but fascinating. El Al planes are different from any other airlines. On my plane there was a group of chasidic Jews *davening* (praying) all the way across. The stewardesses seem to be serving food all the way across the ocean. It's a flying delicatessen. Then, besides, everybody's always walking up and down the aisles — singing, chatting, praying, eating. Fly El Al to Israel — and stand in the aisles for fourteen hours. El Al shows no movies, but what goes on inside the plane is more swinging than any movie you can see anyway.

Israel! Landing at Lod (that's the airfield; it's outside of Tel Aviv) gave me a funny feeling. It has the bustling, restless energy of youth. It's probably hard for you to realize that Israel is so young. After all, you and I never knew a time when there was no Israel. But there probably wouldn't have been an Israel if it had not been for the killing of six million Jews by Hitler in World War II. While Hitler was killing our people (one out of every three Jews in the world), all the nations of the world closed their doors on Jews. Even the United States. It was as if everybody had put up signs saying: "No Jews or Dogs Wanted Here." After the war, Jews were determined that we would never again have to get down on our knees and beg the world to save us. Jews determined to establish a Jewish homeland—a place where any Jew who needed it, anywhere in the world, could come. Thank God!

You've got to see these people to believe it. Israel is like a living United Nations; people of every color in the rainbow — black, brown, yellow, white — all Jews. Hundreds of thousands of Jews have come here from Arab countries. Thousands came here from a country called Yemen, where Jews had lived for centuries in a primitive way of life. These Jews had to be taught how to

77

use forks and knives, how to use indoor toilets, etc. Many more came from Communist Russia and Rumania, where they were mistreated and pushed around. Some came from poverty in lands like India. Some are too old to work. Some are so sick they need a lifetime of medical care. But Israel takes them all. It's amazing. If America had brought in the same percentage of immigrants, our population would be 800 million. I can't help thinking — what if there were no Israel? Where would suffering Jews go? Who would extend a hand to the persecuted? Who would take care of the old, the beaten survivors of Hitler? The fact of a Jewish state has changed the map of the Jewish world. Today Israel and America are the two most important Jewish communities in the world. And, boy, do we need each other!

I didn't like Tel Aviv too much — it's like a little New York City, all hustle and bustle and noise and people. But Jerusalem, Deb, ah, that's a different story! I think it's the most beautiful city in the world. Pink mountains surround the city. The sky is the bluest sky in the world. The air is clear and clean. My first Friday here I was taken on the Sabbath walking tour to see the ancient synagogues. It's something to realize that King David walked this city, that Solomon built the Western Wall (part of which still stands), and that the prophets spoke to the people right on these grounds. It's a mystical feeling. And it affects the people, too. There is a calm, a serenity, a graciousness about Jerusalem that makes you forget there is still occasional Arab terrorism here. In fact, a large grocery store was bombed by a terrorist during my second day here. Don't tell Mom; she'll worry. The Israelis don't seem to be one bit afraid. They have so much self-confidence. Me, I worry.

But I love it here. Miss you. Love to all. I'm growing a

full-length, rabbinic beard — don't tell Dad, he disapproves.

Y.M. in J.

Dear Deb,

Your Man in Jerusalem is safe, sound, and happy. I'm now enrolled in an Ulpan — that's a special program to learn Hebrew. I'm not doing so well, so far, but I'll get there. If you get a chance to learn Hebrew, don't throw the opportunity away. I now wish I had attended the afternoon Hebrew courses at the JCC. Israel is much more fun if you can speak the language. Otherwise, you're a tourist — with camera, questions, the whole bit.

Yesterday I was taken to visit a kibbutz. Do you know what a kibbutz is? Well, it's a collective settlement. Now do you know what it is? Well, anyway, it's like a large farm, with lots of families living and working on it, but everybody owns everything together. Nobody gets money. Everybody has all his needs — food, shelter, clothing, etc. — taken care of by the kibbutz. It reminds me a little of a UAHC camp in the states. Only the kibbutz is a permanent way of life, not just a summer experience. Instead of competition, which is the way our economy operates in the United States, the kibbutz is built on cooperation. Nobody gets rich and nobody is poor. If the kibbutz flourishes, they buy new farm equipment, trucks, put up a new culture hall or something like that. One of the most unusual things is that young children are not raised in their parents' homes on the kibbutz. They are raised in the central nursery. They visit with their parents a couple of times each day. But they have their meals at the nursery. The grown-ups in the kibbutz do physical labor—working the fields, taking care of the animals, working in the orchard, washing dishes, etc. Everybody eats together in the large dining hall. It is so different from our lives back home. There, the family is the central unit. Here, the community — the kibbutz — is the central unit. What's your reaction to it?

I talked to one of the elected leaders of the kibbutz, Zvi Dafni. He has lived in this kibbutz for thirty-five years (it was organized before the state was born). He was a pioneer. He recalled how he and the other founders had to clear the malarial swamps to get the kibbutz started. He himself caught malaria, but he recovered. Half the founders died the first year. What guts they must have had. Most of them came from Russia. They had never done physical labor before. They knew nothing about farming. Arab gangs attacked them constantly; every kibbutznik had to carry a gun along with a shovel or rake. And, yet, they built this kibbutz which is now one of the most successful in Israel. In addition to farming, they now have a factory within the kibbutz to make transistor radios.

But the kibbutz movement has its problems, too. Many of the children don't come back after their tour of duty in the army (everybody must serve — girls and boys). Zvi looked so sad when he told me about his own son. "In your country, you say 'how're they going to keep them down on the farm after they've seen New York.' Well, we have the same *tsore* [trouble]. Many of the youngsters want the excitement of Tel Aviv, or of a frontier town like Elath. Some of them get tired of group living. Some want to make money. Some want to become doctors or professional soldiers or lawyers. I can't blame them, but what kind of future does the kibbutz have if our own children run away? To us, this is a more meaningful way of life — cooperative, hard working, satisfying. We feel that this life is superior to the rat-race, the me-first, money-grubbing, selfish life of the city. The question is: How will you spend your life? Where would Israel be without the kibbutz movement which has provided most of the political leaders of the State? Take David Ben-Gurion. When he finished as prime minister, what did he do? He went back to his kibbutz at Sde Boker."

The kibbutz idea intrigues me. I wonder if I would enjoy that kind of life. Would I miss the privacy of ordinary life? Would I get sick and tired of the physical labor, the sweating? Would cleaning chicken coops become a drag after a while? I don't know. But it makes me remember some dumb conversations at college in the states where some of the "radical" kids used to condemn Israel and cry crocodile tears about the poor "socialist" Arab countries. What hogwash! Saudi Arabia still practices slavery. Egypt, Syria, and Jordan are still feudal regimes. The only democracy in this whole part of the world is Israel. And as for really radical ideas, the kibbutz is one of the most exciting experiments in economic and human relations in the world. You should see the students from African countries studying the way the kibbutz operates. The idea of collective life has gone haywire in Russia and communist countries. But it is working in Israel, one of the few real laboratories for new ways of living together.

Now the Reform Jewish movement has started the Kibbutz Yahel in the Negev. Jewish kids from the United States, Canada, and Israel are developing a unique kibbutz, combining Zionist ideals and the ideals of Reform Judaism. What a challenge! To build the land and to build their own Jewish lives. How would you like to commit your life to such an adventure? Does the idea of aliyah turn you on as it does me? Write already. The only letter I got from you was that kooky one about your birthday party. Love and kisses.

Y.M. in J.

Dear Deb,

Hey, did I tell you about my roommate? A groovy kid from Milwaukee named Carl. He's smart as a whip, for which I am a little sorry because he makes me feel like some kind of an idiot. Carl is thinking of becoming a rabbi. He's very religious. He never seems to study, but he sails through his tests like the Israeli army through the Sinai. Anyway, Carl is real great, but yesterday he and I had our first big quarrel. It was nothing personal. It was about Israel.

Carl and I had just come out of our psych lecture and we headed for the cafeteria for a cup of coffee. Everybody was scurrying around in excitement and confusion. The cafeteria had just been bombed. More than twenty students were injured. The cafeteria was a wreck. Soldiers and policemen poured onto the campus. It really brought the war close to us. When I saw all the kids being loaded into ambulances, I got furious. "Damn those Arabs," I said, "I hope we hit them back twice as hard!"

Carl gave me a very funny look. "Listen, Chuck, I'm as upset as you are. This is a horrible, bloody crime. But do two wrongs make a right?"

"Are you kidding?" I yelled at him. "What are we supposed to do? Turn the other cheek? Congratulate the Arabs for their fine terror work? Sit around and pray?"

"Chuck, bloodshed is not the Jewish way. The Bible teaches that 'vengeance is the Lord's.' That means that vengeance is not for man, but for God. And we also believe that 'Not my might, or by power, but by Thy

82

Spirit, saith the Lord.' What does that mean anyway?"

"Oh, the Bible teaches many things which aren't always practical. It says you shall not kill. But didn't Israel have to fight for its life when the Arabs attacked in war and tried to push the Jews into the sea? It says we should love our enemies — a nutty idea. I think you're crazy. Do you expect Israel to sit by and let bloodthirsty people destroy them?"

"Chuck, I'm not saying that it's easy not to hit back. It's easier to hit back. I admit that any other country would hit back immediately. But Israel shouldn't. We should protest to the United Nations, appeal to the conscience of the world, but we shouldn't answer blood with blood."

Now we were really shouting at each other. "Do you expect us to be angels, saints? We're only human. Are we supposed to be better than anybody else?"

"The answer to that, Chuck, is yes. That's why we took the Ten Commandments from God. That's why the Jewish people entered into a covenant with God. To be a holy people. A different people. Not to be the same. But to be moral, to be good, to be more human, more spiritual. What good is our having a Jewish state if it will spill blood and resort to violence like any other state?"

"Carl, you're unreal. You know Israel has appealed to the United Nations every time the Arabs have blown up innocent women and children, shelled kibbutzim, mined our roads. What good did it do? The U.N. has never done a thing about it. The only thing that ever stopped the Arabs even for a short time was a reprisal, a raid, a bloody nose. That's the only thing the Arabs understand! I can't believe you really mean what you're saying!"

Now Carl was so excited he could hardly talk. "Chuck, don't you understand what you are doing? I mean, we believe in one God and one brotherhood of man, don't we? Then aren't Arabs also the children of God? Aren't they also our brothers? And how can you talk about them as if they are all of one kind — all terrorists and savages. There are good Arabs and bad Arabs as there are good Jews and bad Jews. But when any group is all lumped together, whether it is blacks or Jews or Arabs, you are guilty of bigotry, of group labeling. And what good will it do if Israel now goes into Arab cities and blows up one of their schools? Then the Arabs will come back with another and bigger bombing! Every attack will mean a counterattack. What good is that?"

"But, Carl, what choice do we have? Are we supposed to just stand there and be led to our slaughter the way the Jews in Hitler's Europe did? You don't understand the Israelis. They are ashamed that Jews went quietly to their gas ovens in Europe. They won't do that! They will fight! That's what they mean when they say: 'No More Auschwitz!'"

"Oh, I know about that! But I also know that our Hebrew prophets were the first to bring the world the idea of universal peace, where men will beat their swords into plowshares. It's easy to hit back. It's harder to figure out how to achieve peace. We've got to break through the wall of hate between the Arabs and Israelis. We've got to use our imagination to communicate with them, to reach them, to build understanding. Otherwise, we will all be destroyed and maybe the whole world with us."

"Carl, you're living in a dream world. The real world is not ready for the teachings of the Bible. And are Jews supposed to be the only ones who take the Ten Commandments seriously? Are we always to be the victims, the people who perish? I won't buy that. Neither will the Israelis. We will hit them back every time they hit us.

84

Look, nobody wants peace more than Israel does. This country is not militarist. They fight when they have to, but they would want nothing better than to live in peace with their neighbors. But you must get this through your head. The Arabs refuse to even talk to us. They won't negotiate. They won't even recognize our right to live. So Israel has no choice — *ein brera!*"

"No, no, no, Chuck. Sometimes more can be achieved by nonviolence, by not hitting back, by not lowering yourself to your opponent. Martin Luther King, Jr., never hit back, even when he was spat upon, beat up, arrested, stabbed. And he achieved more for black rights than the Black Panthers and other violent groups will ever achieve."

"But King was an individual. How can you expect a nation to adopt a policy of nonviolence in a violent world? Israel's first obligation is to survive. To live. Jews all over the world must have an Israel. And the only way it can live is to defend itself, its borders, its people. I hope we will hit them so hard they will think twice before doing this again."

Carl said, "I hope we will have the strength and the courage not to hit back! And it's a good thing I'm nonviolent or I'd belt you one right in the nose!"

Well, that was the argument. Who do you think was right? What would you have said if you were with us? Write already! Love.

Y.M. in J.

Projects

Recently a famous psychiatrist went to Israel to make a study of the kibbutz. How does kibbutz life affect the children? Would these Jewish youngsters turn out much different than Jewish children raised in private homes in the cities? In other words, did the kibbutz system work?

Dr. Bruno Bettelheim answered these questions in his book, *The Children of the Dream.* Before he did his study, the doctor suspected that the children of the kibbutz would grow up disturbed because their parents seemed to have rejected their roles as mothers and fathers and turned the children over to a group nursery on the kibbutz for care. Wouldn't these kids show the bad effects of not enough love and attention from parents? The answer was no. The children grew up healthy, happy, and strong. Dr. Bettelheim concluded that what the youngsters had not gotten from their parents, they got from each other, from the powerful sense of group, from the very idea of kibbutz.

The doctor found that, since their parents were rarely around, this removed the need for the children to compete against each other for adult attention. Because there was not the separation between "home" and "community" we have in our society, the kibbutz children were able to relate to each other easily. The youngsters felt themselves a part of the total group and knew that "the seed they plant today becomes the orchard of tomorrow." They flourished in the combined tasks of school, work, and such physical work as gardening, carpentering, and harvesting.

Instead of the parents setting forth a code of behavior — right and wrong — in the kibbutz these standards tended to be set by the group itself. The goal is cooperation, not competition. Can you imagine yourself living and working on a kibbutz?

Dr. Bettelheim proved that the kibbutz experience created a new and different personality. Almost none of the kibbutzniks engaged in crime or juvenile delinquency or drugs and very few had mental troubles. Moreover, the kibbutzniks contribute many leaders to the government of Israel and to the army. Kibbutzniks provided many of the heroes of the Six Day War.

But Dr. Bettelheim also found some bad effects of the

kibbutz. He found that the kibbutz youngsters knew how to get along well in groups, but not as well in close person-to-person relations. They did not seem to be comfortable when alone. They did not have as much ability as nonkibbutz children in thinking for themselves and coming up with independent ideas. Therefore, the kibbutzim have produced few artists, writers, and thinkers. They have instead produced men and women of action. Can you understand why? Is this an important failing in kibbutz life?

Despite this, the doctor concluded that the kibbutz idea is one of the most important experiments in human relations in the world. He suggests that the kibbutz idea could be used in America to solve the problems of our slums. Can you imagine what he has in mind?

The doctor thinks that America's Headstart Anti-Poverty program, in which deprived children get preschool educational programs to try to make up for their poor home life, puts too much strain on each child. He has to live in two worlds — school and home — and the two are too different. In the kibbutz, on the other hand, children spend their entire lives in a creative group environment rather than with their own parents, who perhaps are illiterate and live under bad conditions. They come to accept all the children as their brothers and sisters. Studies show that little Jewish children who came to Israel from Yemen and North Africa — and who could not read or write and were terribly deprived — gained 25 or more points in their intelligence quotient after a few years of life in an Israeli kibbutz.

Do you agree that the kibbutz idea could be used in America to help solve our racial and slum problems? How could we go about it?

1. On the subject of the kibbutz you can:

(a) Read more about the kibbutz in A. Segal and H. Essrig's *Israel Today* (New York: Union of American Hebrew Congregations, new edition, 1977).

(b) Invite an ex-kibbutznik—or someone who has spent time living on a kibbutz — to speak to the class.

(c) Establish a pen-pal correspondence with a child your age who lives on a kibbutz.

(d) Show a film on kibbutz life.

(e) Write an imaginary letter to Dr. Bruno Bettelheim, commenting on his ideas in *Children of the Dream,* as de-

87

scribed in this chapter.

(f) Make up a story of what it would be like to be a kibbutznik.

(g) Write to the Jewish Agency, 515 Park Avenue, New York, New York 10022, for pictures and materials to make up a kibbutz scrapbook.

(h) Make a drawing or painting of a kibbutz as you imagine it.

(i) Best of all — visit a kibbutz in Israel and write a report about it for *Keeping Posted.*

2. Debate:

(a) Israel Should Not Practice Reprisals Against Arab Terror."

(b) "The Kibbutz Idea Could Help to Solve America's Slum Problems."

3. Do a report on the problem of the Arab refugees. Write to the UAHC, Publications Dept., 838 Fifth Avenue, New York, N.Y. 10021, for material.

4. Do a report on Reform Judaism in Israel and find out about the Leo Baeck School in Haifa. Write to the World Union for Progressive Judaism, 838 Fifth Avenue, New York, N.Y. 10021.

5. Act out the argument between Carl and Chuck. Assign the parts to two students. Continue the discussion. Let the class be the jury to decide who is right.

6. Organize a program of buying trees in the UAHC forest in Israel. Write to the UAHC for information; their address is above.

7. Write to the UAHC, Reform Kibbutz, for information on Kibbutz Yahel.

6.

The Silent Jews of Russia

It felt strange to get a letter from a cousin I had never met. It felt even stranger to know that my cousin lived so far away in Moscow, Russia, and that the letter had been handed by my cousin to some friends of my parents who had been tourists in Russia. I felt as if I were reading a secret, smuggled document from the communist world and, in a sense, I was.

Dear Marc,

Please forgive me my English, it is not so good, I learn at my school in Moscow. I send this letter by hand through your friends because I am afraid to write so frankly in the mail. I and my family embrace you and kiss you and pray that we will see each other some day soon and that you and I will become friends.

I tell you about the life of myself and my family. We live in Moscow in a small but pleasant flat. Father is a chemist, mother is a teacher at Moscow University. Grandfather is not well and he lives with us too. It is crowded but we are of good fortune to have a bathroom of our own, a refrigerator, and a television set. Last week we saw the cosmonauts, and we were very proud along with all other Russians. You are also proud of your astronauts. We have also a record player and I listen to Western records, rock and roll, and jazz which my parents do not approve and wish I would cease. Do you like such music? Please to write me about it.

Out material situation is not bad. We have enough to live all right. It is our treatment as Jews we worry about. Last week a Jewish young man tried to give up his Soviet citizenship and demanded the right to go to Israel. He made public statement that, if the regime insists on mistreating him because he is a Jew, he demands the right to live a full Jewish life which he cannot now do in Soviet Union. In the old days of Stalin, he would be shot for that. Now no, but it still takes courage to do it. I would not have that courage. But I sympathize with him.

We are not allowed to live as Jews in the way other religious and nationality groups in Russia are allowed to live. No Jewish schools, no Jewish theatre, no seminary to train rabbis, no real Jewish organizations, no contact with our fellow Jews in other countries in the world, no Jewish books. And since the Israel war, the newspapers are full of terrible words calling Israel a Nazi state and warning us not to express any interest or sympathy for Israel. The Soviet Union, you know well, has elected to arm the Arabs to destroy Israel. If the government opened the gates to its Jews, who knows how many of the three million of us here would vanish overnight. If they do not want us, why do they not let us go?

It is so strange. We are not a religious family, except for grandfather who goes regularly to the Great Synagogue in Moscow. How could we be religious, we who were brought up on atheism [the belief there is no God]? We are modern, believing socialists. Then would you not imagine that, after all these generations, we would stop being Jews? By now, should not the last flicker of Jewishness have died out? But no, it is not so. Our people in Israel are always in our hopes and prayers. So are you, our beloved relatives in the United States. And when an Israeli artist appears at the concert hall, so many Jews rush to get tickets that it is sold out in hours. And we sit there with our hearts in our mouths, our spirits soaring,

90

even though, can you believe, we children do not understand a word of Yiddish or Hebrew. What is it then? A miracle? But I do not believe in miracles. Yet it is so strange.

And in the same way, once a year, on Simchat Torah, we all join so many young Jews who sing and dance outside the synagogue. Even my Jewish friends who are active members of the Komsomol [Communist Youth] come. Last year there were thirty thousand of us, dancing and crying, singing and laughing. It must make the authorities to think. I cannot explain it myself. I think maybe the regime wants to blot out our Jewishness and we will not let them. We do not really know what it is to be Jews and they do not permit us to find out, but it is like we choose to hold on to the memory and the feeling. We must not give them a victory. Our enemies have had enough victories over us. This is why I and my family went to the synagogue the day after the Six Day War to give thanks that Israel had triumphed. We are entitled to that.

I hope that you and all Jews outside of the Soviet Union will continue to protest against the way we Jews are treated by our own government. The Soviet leaders do not like to look like anti-Semites and barbarians before the world. They are nervous about world opinion. So please cry out, petition your government, influence the leaders of the world to protest. Only you can speak for us. We cannot speak for ourselves. You are our tongue and our hope.

Again, I embrace you and your loved ones.

Andrei

I had not known much about the problems of Soviet Jews until I got the letter from my cousin Andrei. The rabbi had talked about it a couple of times and there was some stuff in *Keeping Posted*. But Andrei made it real. My own cousin! I decided to find out all I could about the problem so I could do something intelligent about it. I found out that all Soviet Jewish adults have the word "Yevrei" on their identification papers which must be carried by all Soviet citizens. I found out that anti-Semitism was against the Russian constitution, but I found out that was just ignored. There are quotas limiting the number of Jews who can go to certain schools. Jews are kept out of high positions in the Communist Party and the government. I learned that Jews are named publicly as Jews when they are arrested for so-called "economic crimes" and that such crimes (smuggling, embezzling, etc.) can be punished by death in the Soviet Union. Jews are not allowed to move out of the Soviet Union, except in rare cases. There are only a handful of rabbis in the whole Soviet Union and they are not permitted to go to international conventions with other Jewish leaders from other countries. Other religious and nationality groups in Russia have their own national associations and are able to contact their co-religionists abroad. The few rabbis are very old. No young men are being trained. What will happen when these rabbis die?

Once I knew some of the facts, I tried to find out what can be done to help the Jews of Russia. I found that Andrei was right — only the power of world public opinion could change the situation of Soviet Jews. The Soviet Union of today is not the same as the Soviet Union of Stalin's day. Today the Soviets are eager to be accepted as a civilized society by the world, especially by the United States. The way the Soviets treat their own Jewish citizens is bad news around the world — and bad propaganda for the Soviet Union. The Russians like to hold themselves out to the nations of the world as champions of justice and progress. They give themselves a black eye when they are revealed as old-fashioned anti-Semites. Therefore, it is important to show the world that the Soviets are putting down Jewish religious and cultural life. This protest is gathering. Some of the greatest intellectuals of the world — as well as some communist parties in the West — have condemned the Soviet Union's mistreatment of its Jewish citizens. These mounting protests have already done a little good. Now it is easier for Soviet Jews to get matzoh at Passover time; a few Yiddish and Hebrew books are now being published; some of the ugliest anti-Semitic books have been removed; and a few more Jewish families in the Soviet Union have been allowed to leave Russia to go to Israel or the United States. But much more remains to be done.

Projects

1. It was a brief item in the synagogue bulletin: "Members of the congregation are urged to join in a public demonstration of protest against Soviet policy toward its Jewish citizens. All synagogues and Jewish organizations in the community are participating. The mayor, other important public officials and Christian religious leaders will be with us. Raise your voice in behalf of three million of our fellow Jews. The demonstration and march will take place Sunday, ———at———Park. Jews in Russia cannot speak for themselves. Let us not fail to speak for them!"

Jerry Ash brought the synagogue bulletin to the meeting of the youth group. "I propose that the entire youth group join in the rally and that we march under our own picket signs."

Hedi Diamond disagreed. "I'm against that suggestion. In the first place, I don't think we know the facts about the situation of Jews in Russia. I mean, my father saw that item in the synagogue bulletin and he blew his cool. He said it's ridiculous. The Russians are against all religions; they're atheists, so naturally they're against the Jewish religion, too. And there is freedom for nobody in the Soviet Union, so how can we expect it for Jews?"

"Come off it, Hedi," said Jerry. "After all, the rabbis and all our Jewish leaders have studied this. They've looked into the facts and they are all behind this rally. They all feel that Jews in Russia are singled out for special treatment, above and beyond what everybody else there is given."

"But, Jerry, just because our leaders say that doesn't make it true."

"No," Jerry retorted, "but it doesn't make it untrue either, does it?"

Karen got into the argument. "Look, I don't know the facts and I don't think you do either. But I agree with Hedi that we should stay out, but for a different reason. If things are bad for Jews over there, what good is it going to do for people to march over here? How do we know it won't just make matters worse for them?"

Several of the young people began to speak at once, but Jerry's angry voice drowned them out: *"I'll bet that some Jews in this country said exactly the same thing when Jews in Germany were being slaughtered by Hitler.* You heard the Russians putting down Israel and the Jews at the United Nations. What are we supposed to do? Just sit around on our hands? Or pray that things will get better? I don't care whether you want to march or not. I'll be there. I think it's the least I can do."

The meeting broke up in a hassle. Trying to save the meeting, the chairman announced that he was forming two subcommittees. The first is to study whatever material is available as to the facts on Soviet Jews. The second is to bring in a report as to whether or not the group should participate in the rally. As a member of the group, you can serve on either subcommittee.

Subcommittee 1 can secure a print of the film, *The Price of Silence,* a documentary on Soviet treatment of its Jewish citizens, from the Jewish Chautauqua Society, 838 Fifth

Avenue, New York, N.Y. 10021, for showing to the youth group. It can also get material from the American Jewish Conference on Soviet Jewry, the American Jewish Committee, the Anti-Defamation League, and the UAHC.

Subcommittee 2 should base its report on a discussion as to whether public protest has had any effect on Soviet policy thus far, and whether such campaigns have been helpful or hurtful in similar situations, perhaps even including the Hitler era. To assist in this, interview the rabbi, other Jewish community leaders who are familiar with the problem, and write to the National Jewish Community Relations Advisory Council, 55 W. 42nd St., New York, N.Y. 10036, a Jewish coordinating agency, to see what evidence they have either way.

Both subcommittees should report at an early meeting, after which the entire youth group should make a decision. You are a member of the subcommittee and of the youth group. Decide!

2. Below is a special prayer entitled the "Matzoh of Hope." You can mimeograph copies of this prayer and mail them to every member of the congregation so they can read this prayer at the Passover Seder. Can you think of why Passover is an appropriate time to remember our Soviet Jewish brothers?

3. Plan an assembly program on Soviety Jewry and, if it is good enough, see if it could be presented to the entire congregation at a Sabbath service.

The National Conference on Soviet Jewry, an association of thirty-eight national American Jewish organizations and over 200 local community councils and federations, seeking the elimination of the wrongs inflicted on Russian Jews by the Soviet government, urges that the following statement be read at the Seder of every American Jewish household.

The leader of the service adds the following comments when distributing the matzah after the blessing. He lifts the matzah, sets it aside, and says:

THIS IS THE MATZAH OF HOPE

This matzah, which we set aside as a symbol of hope for the three million Jews of the Soviet Union, reminds us of the indestructible link that exists between us.

As we observe this festival of freedom, we know that Soviet Jews are not free to learn of their Jewish past, to hand it down to their children. They cannot learn the languages of their fathers. They cannot teach their children to be the teachers, the rabbis of future generations.

They can only sit in silence and become invisible. We shall be their voice, and our voices shall be joined by thousands of men of conscience aroused by the wrongs suffered by Soviet Jews. Then shall they know that they have not been forgotten, and they that sit in darkness shall yet see a great light.

4. A large proportion of Soviet Jews are going to the United States and Canada instead of Israel. Why do you think that is? Is that good or bad? Invite a Soviet Jew — or an expert on the subject from the community — to discuss it with you.

5. Organize a project to help Soviet Jews in your community.

7. Freedom of Speech

Your father is a lawyer. At the dinner table, he sometimes tells you about his cases. Sometimes they're very
boring and sometimes you can't understand him anyway, so you just turn off the conversation. Once in a
while he describes a case that is really groovy, like the fat
lady who sued the hotel because she got stuck in the
bathtub.

Last night Dad hardly said a word during dinner.
Mom prompted him a little: "Anything interesting happen at the office, dear?" He just grunted. Finally, over
coffee, he blurted out: "I've got me a real tiger by the tail.
Guess who came to me today and asked me to defend him
in court?"

"Who?"

"Jacques Fosh, that's who!" he said, watching as
Mom's face registered amazement.

"No!" she exclaimed. "Why should *he* come to *you*?"

"Who's Jacques Fosh?" you broke in.

"Jacques Fosh," Mom said, "is a terrible anti-Semite.
He has a gang of bigots who dress up in old Nazi
uniforms and make speeches against the Jews. He's an
awful, hateful man."

"What's an anti-Semite?" you asked.

"That's somebody who hates Jews just because they're
Jews," Mom replied.

"Well, if he hates Jews," you asked, puzzled, "why did
he come to Dad? Doesn't he know you're Jewish or
what?"

"Why shouldn't he come to me?" Dad replied. "He
knows I'm a good lawyer and he knows that I go to bat

97

for anybody whose right to free speech is taken away from him."

"You couldn't!" sputtered Mom. "You couldn't go to court and defend an out-and-out Jew-hater like Fosh! Are you getting soft in the head, Nat? Or are you putting us on?"

"No, darling, I'm dead serious. I didn't say yes, but I didn't say no. I just don't know what to do. After all, a lawyer doesn't have to agree with his client in order to defend his rights. I mean, I've defended murderers, communists, Birchites, embezzlers, sex maniacs, the works. Everybody is entitled to a lawyer, you know. The question is: On what basis can I refuse to represent Fosh?"

"What do you mean 'on what basis?'" Mom demanded. "Any basis! Listen, how would it look in the papers — Nat Goldstone, attorney and leader in many Jewish causes, is defending Jacques Fosh, one of the worst anti-Semites in America. It's ridiculous, Nat! You just tell him to drop dead! You don't need that kind of slimy business." She paused, then added: "Can you imagine what the kids in school would say to Debby and what the girls in the Sisterhood will say to me? It's crazy!"

Dad stirred his coffee thoughtfully. "I know it would be misunderstood. But that's not the important point for me. If you can't stand the heat, you should stay out of the kitchen. I believe that the Constitution of the United States protects every person's right to say what he thinks. It's easy to protect the rights of those who think the way we do. The real test is whether we will stand up for the rights of those whose ideas we hate — the communists, the racists, the Birchites, atheists, and even anti-Semites. Let me ask you, darling, isn't an anti-

98

Semite entitled to a lawyer?"

"He's entitled to choke, as far as I'm concerned," Mom said angrily, as she began to clear the dishes.

"*You* can talk that way, Esther. But I'm a lawyer. The man has been denied use of the public park for a speech. I think that goes against the Constitution. Isn't he entitled to a lawyer to defend his rights?"

"Oh, maybe," Mom replied from the kitchen. "But there's no law that says it must be *you*. The woods are full of lawyers. You have the right to pick your clients. I mean, you're a free man, too, or aren't you?"

"Yes, of course, I could simply say no. And I might do just that. I don't know. But, look, it's not illegal to express prejudiced views, disgusting as they are. It's only illegal if you act on your bigotry. Like beating somebody up, or starting a riot, or trespassing on property, or refusing to hire somebody, or refusing to sell a house to somebody purely because of his race or religion. And if they can deny Fosh his right to speak, they can deny that right to anybody whose views are not popular — and then where are we? Would we still be a free nation?"

"I don't get it," you break in. "You mean it's okay for any nut to get up and say bad things about Jews or Catholics or blacks or whatever? Why don't they make a law against that?"

"You don't understand, Debby," Dad said. "The Constitution won't let you pass a law against what people *say*, only against what people *do*. And, anyway, who would be the judge of which statements are kosher and which are not? It's impossible. Do you understand?"

"No," you said, honestly.

"And me neither," shouted Mom. "I mean Hitler only talked at first, too, and pretty soon his crazy talk whipped up all those nuts and hoods and they beat up

99

Jews and took over Germany and killed six million Jews and almost took over the whole world. You and all those other lawyers are so wrapped up in that Constitution that the Nazis will take over here, too. You and all that free speech jazz. Doesn't wild talk lead to action? Doesn't it?"

"Sometimes yes, sometimes no. If it leads to disorder and violence, the law must step in. If somebody cries 'fire' in a crowded theater, he should be arrested. But the law must protect the right of even the most vicious and prejudiced guy to say his piece."

Mom screwed up her face and silently shook her head in disagreement with Dad's arguments.

"Esther, my love, it is not hard to see where you stand. But I hereby entrust the decision to Your Honor, Debby Goldstone. What do you say, Deb? Do I take the case or don't I?"

What would you say if you were Deb?

Jews have always been strong supporters of free speech. Why do you think this is? For one thing, Jews have always felt that learning is one of the most important values. You cannot have real learning unless people are free to look at all ideas. Even when Jews in the Middle Ages were kept behind the walls of dingy ghettos, they always saw to it that their children were well educated. These ghetto Jews were poor and mistreated, but their learning was much greater than that of the Gentiles who penned them in. Jews are known as the People of the Book not only because of our love for the Bible, but for our love of learning.

When you study the Bible, you will see free speech in action. You will see the prophets and others saying unpopular things which made powerful persons very

100

angry. The prophet Nathan put down King David because the king stole Bathsheba from her husband. Elijah publicly dressed down King Ahab for his behavior. Job even talked back to God. These are just a few examples of people free to express their thoughts and their consciences in Jewish history. The prophets could not have spoken freely and their message would not have been preserved had their society not honored free speech.

After the destruction of the Temple, Jews began to draw up the Talmud. When there was a difference of opinion among the rabbis, the sages just put both opinions — the majority as well as the minority — into the Talmud. This was because Jews respected themselves and each other, and you cannot respect another person unless you also respect his ideas, even those ideas you do not accept.

Of course Jews are not angels. There were some times in ancient days — and in our time, too — when Jews with "strange" ideas were prevented from saying their piece. Jeremiah, the great prophet, was sentenced to die as a traitor because he condemned a war the Jewish people were fighting. The prophet Amos was also given a hard time because his views irritated the powers that be. Yet, with some exceptions, Jews have usually felt that man's right to express himself comes from God and must not be tampered with by men.

Because of this history and tradition, American Jews usually find themselves against people and forces who try to cut down on free speech. Jews have supported such groups as the American Civil Liberties Union, which goes to court to protect freedom of speech even for communists, socialists, atheists, and hippies. In the 1950's, there was a senator named Joseph McCarthy, who started a national campaign against people he called "communists." His campaign got thousands of government workers, teachers, writers, and actors fired from their jobs because he frightened their bosses by accusing these persons of being "communists" or "fellow travelers." It turned out that most of the people he persecuted were not communists at all. They just had ideas and opinions that McCarthy didn't like. For a while, Senator McCarthy had immense power. He was able to destroy people just by publicly accusing them of being disloyal to their country. He didn't give them a chance to answer back, nor did he have proof to back up his charges. But the country was so frightened that they were ready to fire almost anybody he accused. A few decent and loyal Americans were so hurt by Senator McCarthy's cruel campaign that they committed suicide. It was a very dark period for all Americans.

Many Americans became afraid to express their ideas. Most Jews were against McCarthy. They believed that he was weakening the United States Constitution, wrecking freedom of speech and spreading suspicion and hate among all Americans. Jews remembered the teachings of Judaism: "Be more careful of thy neighbor's honor rather than of thine own person" (*Zohar Chadash*). Finally, after much damage, the American public got wise to this man and the Senate voted to censure him. Censure means that they condemned him for what he had done. Not long thereafter, Senator McCarthy died. America got back to its senses and to its belief in free speech for everybody.

Yet, like all other freedoms, free speech doesn't give anyone the right to say absolutely anything at any time. There are some limits. Can you think of an example?

How about this? The Supreme Court has said that no one would have the right to yell "fire" in a crowded

102

theater. Why not? Do you agree with the Court?

Once, the Metropolitan Museum of Art in New York City had an exhibit about Harlem. The catalogue for the art show contained an article by a young black girl, which included some anti-Jewish statements, including the sentence: "Behind every hurdle that the Afro-American has yet to jump stands the Jew who has already cleared it." Many people, including the mayor of New York City, felt that this was an anti-Jewish statement and should not be included in the catalogue. But the young lady replied that those were her views and freedom of speech gave her the right to express them. If you had been a member of the Board of the Museum, what position would you have taken on this matter?

You can have freedom of speech (and press), but that does not mean that you do not have to suffer penalties if you have harmed somebody by your words. For example, if you wrote an article in a newspaper about some man in your town, and you called him a communist, or a liar, or a thief, or a criminal, you had better be very certain that you are telling the truth and can prove it. Otherwise, you could be sued for libel. Libel means that you have damaged somebody by telling untruths about him in public.

There is a big argument going on now in America as to whether there should be a law which would also make it illegal for a person to libel a whole racial or religious group. In other words, going back to the example of the young girl and the New York museum catalogue, she could not now be sued for libel. The reason is that she libelled a whole group — in this case, Jews — rather than an individual. This means that, as of now, a bigot can write ugly things about blacks, Irish, Jews, Italians, or any other group. Individuals are protected against libel;

103

not groups. If we had a group libel law, such an attack on a group would be against the law. Do you think such a law would be a good idea? Would it hurt free speech? The American Civil Liberties Union, along with most Jewish organizations, are against group libel laws because they think it would be too hard to prove a libel against a group and would have the effect of cutting down on free speech. What do you think?

Or take a different example. Pretend that the drama club in your school has decided to put on "The Merchant of Venice" by Shakespeare. Some of the rabbis in the community protest. They say that the central character, Shylock, is an ugly picture of a Jew and that this play gives vent to the author's anti-Semitism. The principal of the school disagrees: "In the first place, this is a great classic in our literature. In the second place, we believe in free speech." There is a big argument in the newspapers and the kids in school are taking sides on the question. What would you say? If you were a member of the Student Council, how would you vote on this question?

Free speech also has much to do with who should be permitted to teach in a public school. What if a person is an atheist? Should he be allowed to teach? What if he is an Arab who feels that Jews are an evil people who have destroyed the Arab peoples in winning the State of Israel? What if he is a communist who believes that the Russian system is good and the American system is bad? What if he is a member of an extremist organization which feels that our government has been taken over by communists? These are tough questions. But you can see that, while free speech is very important, sometimes limits have to be drawn. In all these cases, if the teacher did not push his ideas upon the students, couldn't we say that he has a right to teach regardless of his own views? But what if he does push his ideas? If he were fired, would that be a violation of free speech? What do you think?

The glory of America is its freedom, particularly freedom of speech and of press. But it is not always easy to decide how far free speech should be allowed to stretch. Millions of Americans once demonstrated against the Vietnam war because they thought it was a bad and wrong war. Millions of other Americans demonstrated in favor of the war. Each group has the right to do so. In totalitarian countries, people would be punished for opposing their government. Few countries in the world would permit such dissent in the middle of a war. That is part of the greatness of America.

But some Americans became so emotional about the war that at times they carried Viet Cong flags, the flags of our enemies in Vietnam. Others have burned American flags. Is this free speech? Should they have been allowed to do that? Other Americans, on both sides, were so angry that they interrupted meetings of people who did not agree with them, sometimes preventing speakers from enjoying free speech. Should free speech ever be allowed to go to the point where it interferes with someone else's free speech?

Some students in a Des Moines high school came to school with black armbands on their arms to express their protest against continued killing in Vietnam. The principal of the school ordered the protesting children not to wear the armbands inside the school. Some of the youngsters felt their right to free expression was being denied by the school ruling. Some parents complained about the ruling. Other parents said the ruling was correct, because otherwise anybody could wear political buttons, signs, armbands, thus creating disunity in the school. What would you have said? Was the principal right? The matter was taken to court and it went all the way to the Supreme Court. What would you guess the Supreme Court decided? The court said that the principal had interfered with the right of free speech of the students. The court said that the rights of children are also covered by the Constitution. So long as the students do not disrupt classes or interfere with others, they have every right to express their beliefs, by word of mouth or by the message of their armbands.

Are there any limits on free speech? Pornography has become a big issue in movies, plays, magazines, and in the streets. Times Square in New York City has become a sordid ruin because of it. Yet those who make it and show it — even using young children — claim that free speech gives them that right. Should society be able to stop such abuses of freedom? How?

Remember that freedom of speech is your sacred right as an American. It is not a favor that somebody grants you. It is set forth in the very first of the Amendments to the Constitution of the United States. You can disagree with the policy of your own government as strongly as you want, so long as your disagreement is limited to speech. When you act, however, it might be a different situation. Sometimes people feel so strongly that a certain law is wrong that they set out to break that law on purpose. That is not free speech; it is civil disobedience. They are two different things. You cannot be punished for free speech. You can very well be punished for civil disobedience. One is legal; the other is illegal.

One of the most interesting stories in the Bible is the story of Daniel. King Nebuchadnezzar ordered all his subjects to bow down to the golden image. Daniel and his friends (Shadrach, Meshach and Abednego) refused (Daniel 3:18). For this they were sentenced to the fiery furnace. Their refusal was one of the first examples of civil disobedience (the refusal to obey a law) in recorded history. Read the story of Daniel in your Bible.

Did Daniel have a right to refuse to obey the law? Why or why not? Are there any times when a person has a right to go against the law? See if you can give examples from modern times.

In Jewish teaching, Jews were always urged to "obey the law of the land" where they lived. The rabbis said that when law breaks down, people destroy each other like fish in the sea.

But, Jews believe that man must obey God before anyone else. "Thou shalt not have any other gods before Me." What happens if there is a conflict between the demand of a ruler (or a government) and the demand of God (or of a person's conscience)? Since the beginning of history, man has had to face this problem. The prophets, especially, gave their first obedience to God. They often refused to obey the laws of kings and governments when they felt these went against God's words.

There have always been demands by society which some men could not accept. The prophet Isaiah opposed Israel's alliances with Assyria and Egypt. Jeremiah, opposing his people's war against Babylon, could not stop his own conscience: "Then there is in my heart as it were a burning fire, shut up in my bones, and I weary myself to hold it in, but I cannot." Jesus refused to yield to the demands of Roman law, forfeiting his life rather than obey. Rabbi Akiba, defying the law of the Romans, preferred to perish in the flames with the words of the Shema on his lips.

In ancient Athens, Socrates told his accusers: "Men of

Athens, I honor and love you ... but I shall never cease from the practice and teaching of philosophy, exhorting anyone whom I meet and saying to him ... from virtue comes every other good, public and private. ..." And Socrates told the court which convicted him for breaking the law of Athens: "I shall never alter my ways, not even if I have to die many times ... for I will obey God rather than you ... and so I bid you farewell."

This nonviolent refusal to obey a law is called civil disobedience. Civil disobedience has played a role in much of American history as well. The colonists, dumping the tea into Boston Harbor, were breaking the British law on purpose. So-called witches were burned at the stake for disobeying the Salem authorities. Before the Civil War, many people in the North wouldn't obey the cruel Fugitive Slave Law, which forced people to return runaway slaves to their masters. During the Mexican War there were many people, including Abraham Lincoln, whose consciences were hurt by what they regarded as an unjust war. One such man was Henry David Thoreau, the writer. In protest against the war, he refused to pay his local taxes. "What are you doing in there, Henry?" asked his friend, Ralph Waldo Emerson, another famous American writer, who visited him at the Concord jail. "What are you doing out there?" Thoreau replied, implying that in a time of evil it is the duty of men of conscience to oppose that evil, whatever the penalty.

In the 1950's, in the United States, a young Protestant minister in Montgomery, Alabama, inspired by Mahatma Gandhi, used similar methods of civil disobedience as a weapon against racial segregation in the south. The minister was Martin Luther King, Jr. He succeeded in touching the conscience of America — and the world — and in striking down many of the cruelties against blacks in the south. For this, King received the Nobel Peace Prize. He later tried to bring civil disobedience into the struggle against racial slums in the north, as well as against the war in Vietnam. He gave his life in the fight for justice.

It is important to make clear what civil disobedience is and what it is not. Civil disobedience is not a right; it is a moral duty a person feels he must in conscience do, no matter how he is punished for it. Civil disobedience is not the same as free speech. Speech is legal and rightful protest; it goes on the belief that education can bring about a desired change in policy. Dissent breaks no law; it comes under the Bill of Rights. Civil disobedience is not necessarily an attack upon the social order. By purposely breaking a law he thinks is bad, a man is showing a faith in society's ability to fix its mistakes. Such a person may be sacrificing himself to show up a moral issue, firm in the belief that by so doing he can lead public opinion to change the law.

There must be certain limits to the practice of civil disobedience in a democracy. It must not be violent, for violence is not disobedience but insurrection. It must not harm other citizens' rights, such as the right to speak, assemble, petition. And the person must be prepared to pay the consequences and accept the penalties of his disobedience.

You might think that it is always the duty of a citizen to obey the law of the land. But what if the law of the land is evil? To take extreme examples — Stalin's Russia, Castro's Cuba, or Hitler's Germany. Should a German citizen have, under all circumstances, obeyed the anti-Jewish laws of Nazi Germany? If he did, he became an accomplice of the Nazi evil. And if enough

109

Germans had stood against the anti-Jewish laws and gone into the streets to demonstrate against them, the killing of six million Jews by Hitler might never have happened. Law is not always just. Law can be inhuman. Conscience can lead you to defy — or evade — laws that are bad. Thus, we do not condemn — indeed, we honor — those who broke the law and saved Jews in occupied Europe in World War II, those whites and blacks who oppose the cruel, anti-black rules in South Africa, those writers and poets who speak the truth in Soviet Russia, even though their government objects.

Yes, you might say, civil disobedience is all right in a country that is not free, where unjust laws cannot be changed by the people. But would it ever be proper in a free, democratic society like the United States? This has become a big issue in American life. For even in America, a law can be unfair. Until recently, the states of the south had laws which separated black and white citizens. Public washrooms, drinking fountains, railroads,, buses, schools, hotels, restaurants — all were segregated, and this segregation was protected by state and local laws. Was it proper or improper to challenge these laws by breaking them? Thousands of Americans, regarding these laws as against their religious and human consciences, organized sit-ins and other demonstrations to get rid of these unfair laws. These challenges went to the United States Supreme Court which, in almost every case, ruled that racial segregation is unconstitutional. These challenges also showed the world the second-class position of the American black in the south and helped persuade the Congress to pass new civil rights legislation, guaranteeing to every American full equality of opportunity.

It is not always easy to draw the line as to when and how civil disobedience is right. (For instance: Do college protestors have the right to occupy a college building?) One thing is clear: People taking this step must accept the consequences of their act of conscience, whether this means prison, social abuse, or some other penalty. Some Americans used civil disobedience against the Vietnam war, refusing to be drafted because they believed the war was wrong. Were they justified? One dramatic example of this was Muhammed Ali (Cassius Clay), world heavyweight champion, who had refused to accept his draft call. Do you consider him a traitor or an American faithful to his own conscience? If you had the power, what would you have done about him?

The Jewish religion is based on law. Respect for law goes deep in Jewish tradition. One of the important Jewish teachings is to respect the rulers and the laws of whatever nation Jews live in. But Judaism also teaches that there is a law which is higher than the law of man. The Law of God is highest. The brotherhood of man is beyond national boundaries and local laws. Patriotism, which can often inspire the finest in men, can also lead to evil. "My country ... right or wrong" can cause terrible things. Why?

In the end, each human being must live with his own conscience. In a free society the state is the servant of the people. If the state makes a mistake, it is our job as citizens to try to correct the error. If in the extreme situation this cannot be done by democratic means, then we must at least respect the conscience of those who feel they have to go to civil disobedience. For let us remember that the law did not permit the ancient Hebrews to flee Pharaoh, or the Maccabees to rise up against the Syr-

111

ians, the American colonists to dump tea into Boston Harbor, or black youngsters to sit at the lunch counters in Greensboro, North Carolina. Conscience is the voice of God and it must be answered.

Projects

1. Invite a representative of the American Civil Liberties Union from your community to tell you about any issues of free speech or free press in your own community.

2. Show a movie on free speech:

(a) *Animal Farm.* Based on George Orwell's famous fable, this is a feature-length cartoon film dealing with the revolt of Farmer Jones' domesticated animals against their cruel master. Once the animals have seized power, they are taken over by the pigs, who are the "shrewdest of the bunch," and the liberated animals soon find that they have succeeded in exchanging one form of tyranny for another and once again are forced to unite in a common cause. Contact: Contemporary Films—McGraw Hill, 1220 Ave. of the Americas, New York, N.Y. 10020.

(b) *Freedom to Read.* A controversy over censorship. Anti-Defamation League, 315 Lexington Avenue, New York, New York 10016.

(c) *Freedom to Learn.* A teacher is charged with communism. ADL (above).

3. Debate:

(a) "There Should Be a Group Libel Law against Defaming Any Religious or Racial Group."

(b) "Emile Zola Berman, a Jewish Lawyer, Should *Not* Have Agreed to Represent Sirhan Sirhan, the Murderer of Robert Kennedy."

(c) "Persons Who Protest against United States Policies Should Be Placed in Detention Centers."

(d) "Atheists (people who do not believe in God) Should

Not Be Allowed to Teach in a Public School."

(e) "A Twelve-Year-Old Should Be Allowed to See *The Graduate* or Any Other Movie He Wishes to See."

4. Pretend you are one of the children in a Des Moines school during the arm-band controversy. Which side would you support?

5. Ask your teacher if you could visit the courthouse for an interesting trial and perhaps meet the judge in his chambers.

6. In Miami in 1969, some 15,000 young people organized a protest against "immorality" in songs, movies, and plays. They said they were sick of so much "filthy" material. Would you have joined or not? Does free speech include the right to be dirty?

7. We are all upset about the riots in the cities and the demonstrations on campuses. Many people think the time has come to smash those who protest. Read the following statement and see if you can figure out who said it, why, and in what election campaign.

"The streets of our country are in turmoil. The universities are filled with students rebelling and rioting. Communists are seeking to destroy our country. Russia is theatening us with her might, and the republic is in danger.

"Yes, danger from within and from without. We need law and order.

"Yes, without law and order, our nation cannot survive. We are laughed at by other nations because of the disorder in our streets caused by the students and the Communists.

"Elect us, and we, we shall restore law and order. We shall by law and order be respected among the nations of the world. Without law and order, our republic shall fall."

The answer is Adolf Hitler, 1932 election speech, Hamburg, Copy out this quote and try it on your friends, parents, and relatives. See how many can answer it correctly. What do you think is the connection between this statement by Hitler and what could happen in America?

113

8. Religious Liberty

Until quite recently the public schools in Miami had a very unusual way of celebrating Christmas. The high point of the celebration was a play giving the main points of the life and death of Jesus, at the school assembly. It was very dramatic. Students played the roles of Jesus, his mother, Pontius Pilate, the Jews (who, according to the play, were responsible for Jesus' death), and the Romans. In the crucifixion scene, the lights were turned off in the auditorium, strong music was played in the background, a spotlight was turned on Jesus as he suffered the last moments of his agony on the cross. To make the acting even more vivid, ketchup was spread on the actor's body, who was dressed only in a loin cloth, and the boy moaned and sobbed. The assembly was compulsory for all students and it had such an effect on some of the children that they cried and, in a few cases, even fainted.

A Jewish organization, the American Jewish Congress, heard about this program and went to court, claiming that such a religious event in the public schools goes against the Constitution. They argued that such a program was unfair to non-Christian children, including Jews, and that it made them feel uncomfortable and unhappy to have to sit through a presentation of religion in conflict with their own beliefs. The American Jewish Congress claimed that religious teaching belongs in the churches and the synagogues and not in the public schools where all children, including even those who do not believe in any religion at all, must be treated as equal citizens. They asked the Supreme Court to stop this

114

practice in Miami — and all other similar religious celebrations in public schools throughout the country — by ruling that such programs go against the First Amendment to the Constitution which says that church and state must be kept separate in the United States. This means religion shouldn't run the government, and the government shouldn't run religion.

Many people, including some Jews, disagreed very strongly with the American Jewish Congress. Some said, "Why make such a big fuss about so little? Besides, the majority of Americans are Christians, so Jews should accept the fact that this is a Christian country and not fight it." Others said, "You'll just get Christians angry at Jews if you get the courts to throw out these programs which are so dear to the hearts and faith of believing Christians." Others said: "It won't hurt those Jewish kids a bit to sit through a Christian program like that. We did it when we were young and we're perfectly good Jews as adults, so why rock the boat so much?"

Which of the two different ideas do you agree with — that of the American Jewish Congress or those who disagreed with its action? Why? Can you think of any other reasons, besides those listed above, for either fighting against the Miami program or going along with it without protest? Pretend you are a student in that Miami school. What would you do about the program? Would you refuse to participate in it? Can you guess what the Supreme Court decided about this case?

The Supreme Court decided that the American Jewish Congress was correct in its idea of what the United States Constitution permits and what it forbids. It ordered the public schools of Miami to remove this program, and it ruled that all public schools must get rid of all religious practices — such as the reading of the

Bible, prayer, and the celebration of the religious aspects of Christmas, Chanukah, and Easter. It said that the child who is an atheist (non-believer in God) has as much right to be a first-class citizen in the public schools as a believing Christian or believing Jew. And, it is interesting to note, the non-Jewish people of Miami, after being a bit upset at first, accepted the decision as the law of the land and there was none of the trouble that was feared.

The question of religion in public education blazed into a national issue in the early 1960's. In June, 1962, the Supreme Court declared that prayer recited in the public schools is unconstitutional. A furious argument resulted. The common reaction was anger at the court. Typical was the statement by the late Cardinal Spellman of New York that the court decision "strikes at the very heart of the godly tradition in which America's children have so long been raised." A southern congressman moaned that "the court put blacks into the schools and has taken God out of them." In the angry backlash against the decision, many traced the court action to the "agitation of a militant and well-organized minority." Such hints usually meant Jews.

Those who hit the court and its decision and said that God had been banished from the public schools forgot a very important segment of American history. They forgot that, in the first half of the nineteenth century, Roman Catholic heads had been broken and violence had stained such cities as New York, Philadelphia, and Boston, when courageous Roman Catholic laymen and clergy fought against Protestant religious practices in the public schools and tried to eliminate Bible reading in the public schools. Indeed, it was these Roman Catholic objections to religious practices in the American public school system which led, finally, to the secular public school system we have today.

Despite the commotion touched off by its prayer decision, the Supreme Court proceeded in June of 1963 to eliminate Bible reading and the Lord's Prayer from public education. The court held that such practices broke the First Amendment of the Constitution and became an illegal "establishment of religion." In the storm which the new decision set off, President John F. Kennedy, America's first Roman Catholic president, calmly called upon the American people to obey the law of the land. He reminded them that they were as free to pray and to worship as they had ever been. He noted, however, that religious faith cannot be forced on anybody. He echoed the truth which had been expressed by the rabbis of old that "prayer without the proper intention [kavanah] is like a body without a soul." In Jewish tradition we are told "make not your prayer a fixed routine but one which is an outpouring of the heart" (Sayings of the Fathers 2:18).

In anger against the Supreme Court, a powerful campaign was launched in the Congress to amend the Constitution to permit prayer and Bible reading in the public schools. For several months, the halls of Congress were filled with appeals to "bring God back into American life," to "reconsecrate" America. It looked as though, out of anger at the court and in the tide of national hysteria, the Congress would tinker and tamper with the Constitution which had served religious liberty so well throughout American history. But sanity won out. Leaders of the National Council of Churches of Christ, representing American Protestantism, together with Jewish leaders of all denominations, and a few distinguished Catholic scholars, appealed to the Con-

117

gress to uphold the court and the Constitution. They explained that, as religious men and women, they did not want religion forced upon a captive audience of public school children. They pointed out that religious belief must come from the heart and not from the school board. And, finally, they succeeded in holding back the tide of public opinion, and the drive to scramble the Constitution ended for a while. It may well heat up again at any time. Meanwhile, we know that many school systems have simply ignored the court decisions and go right on with Bible reading and prayers in the public schools. This is a good way to teach children contempt for law and order!

But the task of keeping church and state separate is a never-ending struggle and it goes forward on many fronts. On several of these fronts there have been major breaks in the wall of separation of church and state.

In recent years, new problems of religious liberty have appeared in America. A number of cults have gotten popular. You have seen — or heard about — several of them, including Hare Krishna, Jews for Jesus, the Unification Church (derisively called the "Moonies"), "I Found It," Hebrew-Christians, and hundreds of others. These groups have a right to religious freedom, granted, but do they have a right to try to convert persons of other faiths into their beliefs? The "Moonies" are accused of bringing people to their institutes for weekends of religious "brainwashing" for the purpose of proselytizing (converting) them. Some say they use fraud and deception by persuading lonely and troubled kids — who may have been on drugs — to enjoy a nice weekend of singing and playing in a warm community in the country. Once there, they are induced to commit themselves to Sun Myung Moon and leave their faith and families.

Many Jewish kids seem to get swept up in the false appeal of these new movements. Why should that be? How is the Jewish community failing such boys and girls who turn their backs on their own synagogue and people and embrace such a strange banner? It is also said that these young people are brainwashed and sometimes their heartbroken parents have gone to court, claiming that the rights of their children were violated. Often the courts have said that persons over 21 have the right to make up their own minds, whether the parents approve or not, even if the religious cult seems crazy and dangerous to most people. The courts have pointed out that most religions started out as small, despised, crazy sects and they have a right to go out and seek converts.

Most ordinary Christian religious groups are as opposed to these new sects as Jews are. They feel they violate Christian teachings. They also say that to try to convert a Jew to another faith is really against true religious liberty. They say one can be a good Christian or a good Jew while respecting the faith of another person whose religious belief is equally precious. What do you think?

But fascinating cases have developed where Jewish parents of a "brainwashed" child are driven to desperation by the fact that their children have been persuaded by a cult to accept Jesus as God. Some of these Jewish kids are foolish enough to believe they can still be good Jews while accepting Jesus as God. Do you agree? What would you say to such a young person? In any event, some of these parents have hired people called "deprogrammers" to kidnap their children and take them to a motel far away for many days of "deprogramming" in an effort to undo the brainwashing.

What is your reaction to this? Is there such a thing as

brainwashing? Could you be persuaded to throw away your Jewish beliefs and accept such ideas? There is now a big argument as to whether forced "deprogramming" is itself legal and right. Most judges so far have said it is against the law to kidnap your own child, no matter what the reason or how heavy the pain. In fact, Ted Patrick — the most famous "deprogrammer" — was put in jail for kidnapping a cult kid at the request of the parents. Do you think it is wrong? What *should* the parents do? What should the Jewish community do? Or is there nothing to do in a free society except to try to strengthen the Jewish ties of our own children so they will not be open to such approaches?

How should a Jewish person feel about Jesus? The answer is: respectfully. Jesus was a good Jew until the day he died. He was not a Christian — his followers created the new religion. Jesus was a Jewish prophet, a teacher, who underwent Bar Mitzvah and observed the Commandments. We do not believe he was God or the Son of God. We believe he was a good and loyal Jewish man. In Jewish teachings, when the Messiah comes, peace and love will fill the world. Obviously war and hate and discord have been humankind's lot since Jesus' time to the present. This is hardly a messianic age and — for us Jews — the terrible truth is that much of the suffering and bloodshed and war have come to the world *in the name of Jesus*, so it is not surprising that no real Jew can ever accept that Jesus was God or the son of God. He was a Jew. . .period!

Projects

1. Debate: "It Would Not Do Any Harm if We Opened the Day in Public School with a Prayer to God."

2. Debate: "An Atheist Should Not Have the Right to Teach in a Public School."

3. In an Illinois town, the public school had a program in which religious teachings were conducted in class. One child refused to participate. The teacher ordered the child to sit in a closet during the religious practice. The child's parents sued the school system. Do you think the child was correct in protesting? Were the parents right to sue?

4. Jehovah's Witnesses do not believe in taking oaths or in saluting flags. It is a matter of conscience with them. Do you think their conscience should be respected or should they be forced to go along with the majority?

5. If the majority of the children in a class are Jewish, should the public school have a right to celebrate Chanukah? Or wouldn't that be just as evil as imposing Christian practices on a Jewish minority? Doesn't separation of church and state mean that Jewish religious practices belong in the home and the synagogue and not in the public school, in the same way that Christian practices belong in the home and the church and not the public school?

6. If there were some things going on in your public school that you thought went against religious liberty for all, how would you go about changing it?

7. Invite a lawyer to tell you about some interesting cases under the First Amendment of the United States Constitution.

8. A very good friend of yours, a Christian, read in the newspapers about the American Jewish Congress' Court case against religion in the public schools. "How come you Jews are against God in the public schools?" he asks you. What do you say in reply?

9. Churches and synagogues do not pay taxes to government. There are those that demand that churches and synagogues be stripped of their tax exemption. What do you think are the main arguments for and against? Give your opinion.

10. Invite an expert to tell your class about the cults like "Moonies" and Hare Krishna and why so many Jews join them.

9. My Parents and I — What Is the Generation Gap?

Dear Editor of the Temple Bulletin:

I've been sitting here attempting to pull together a lot of thoughts concerning my Jewishness and the Jewishness of the father who wrote the letter that was sent to me. It seems to be so difficult for me to relate to that letter, maybe it's because I've been four and a half years in Appalachian Ohio and West Virginia and don't return to all that was our common experience in Miami Beach too frequently, maybe because last week I gave my last five dollars to a family so that they could buy food until their welfare check arrived, or because one of my closest friends is a backwoods minister who believes religion is in the streets and back hollows, or because a friend from Steubenville called me before Thanksgiving to tell me that the churches in his community, including the local synagogue, were withdrawing their financial support from Combat, the local Black Power organization which he worked for, when it began saying publicly that poverty and racism had political and economic origins, or perhaps it's because the synagogues of this country, for all their liberal talk, really practice a very different set of priorities than they preach.

Any institution which claims to be deeply concerned about "civil rights," peace, and poverty, and then spends several million dollars on an architectural face lifting needs to have its priorities rearranged.

I imagine I shouldn't be so harsh because this has been the role of religion traditionally. Is it any wonder that today's youth are turned off. So many of my friends have turned away from organized religion and for good reason.

It is difficult to discuss man's relationship to man in a religious school classroom when the very people who preach it aren't practicing it, their concerns lie, as the father in the letter says, "in a household which practices the Judaism of lighting candles and holding seders," or the Judaism of fund raising for new architecture, and in the Judaism of discussing ethical values instead of trying to make them work.

It becomes silly to single Judaism out, for this is a sickness which affects all of us in this country regardless of religion. It is extremely difficult to really do anything about the problems of racism, peace, and poverty when we are so deeply indebted and entwined within the same political and economic system which keeps these very things going. It even makes the problems very difficult to understand and what kind of role we as individuals or as a group are going to do in seeking their resolution.

Whenever I get to thinking about this subject I'm reminded of an excellent quote from Tolstoy, who said, "I sit on a man's back, choking him and making him carry me, and yet assure myself and others that I am very sorry for him and wish to lighten his load by all possible means — except getting off his back."

Clearly, the Jews of America are in an excellent position to begin to change our talk into action. We are well educated and wealthy enough to begin reevaluating and reorganizing our priorities and goals and we have the historical heritage — for we were once slaves in Egypt. How easily that fact is forgotten, for we are no longer the oppressed. However, for us as Jews, oppression should have a special meaning. Was it not Moses and the Maccabees and many more who demanded that the Egyptians and the Greeks get off our backs.

Today, the poor of the world and our country, in

particular, are demanding the same thing. The poor are no longer content with Civil Rights Acts, Food Stamps, Open Housing, and a myriad of other meaningless laws. (They are demanding that we get off their backs.)

We as Jews should understand that, but we don't. And, much worse, we rationalize a hundred times over why we can't. Again, is it any wonder that the youth of today, Jewish and Christian, are fed up? When will we begin to see the problem for what it is? For, surely, we haven't much more time, for the number of blacks and whites who are willing to change our present system at any cost is increasing everyday. Perhaps the day will come when the synagogues of the United States will contribute to the reorganization of our society instead of helping to make such reorganization necessary.

Sincerely,
Jim

This is a real letter from a Jewish young man who is now working in Appalachia, one of the poorest sections of the United States, as a VISTA volunteer in the anti-poverty program. He attends Ohio University. Jim is a former president of the youth group of his Reform synagogue. Do you understand his letter? In your own words, what do you think he is saying? Do you feel that his case against the synagogue is right or wrong? How would you answer this letter?

Jim is an honest voice of a new generation of young people. He is angry about the kind of world which his parents and others of the older generation left him. Jim obviously believes that human beings are equal and have a right to live in self-respect and dignity. But he sees millions of people, even in wealthy America, living in miserable poverty. Jim obviously believes in human rights for everybody. But he sees an America where black people are confined to slums, shunned by whites and given the leftover crumbs of white society. Jim believes people should live together in peace. But he sees war following war, and all mankind living in the dark shadow of a possible nuclear suicide. Jim believes that religion should help make the world better, but he sees churches and synagogues which seem to care most about new buildings, fund-raising drives and social standing in the community.

Jim is angry. He is so angry he is almost rude. But Jim speaks for millions of young Americans. Many of them are Christians. Many are blacks. Many, like Jim, are Jewish. But all of them are unwilling to accept things as they are. They want to change America and the world. They want to correct the evils they see all around them. They do not want to follow in the footsteps of an older generation which seems, to them, to care more about acquiring things like cars and color television than about establishing justice in our society.

Some of the young people, who feel as Jim does, have given up. One of Jim's best friends in grade school was Marc. When Marc entered high school, he began to experiment with drugs. He smoked marijuana. He once tried L.S.D. Jim learned what Marc was doing and he begged him to stop. "It's illegal. You'll get caught and you'll be thrown out of school and maybe even worse. You'll wreck your life." Marc just laughed at his friend. "Listen, Jimmy boy, this is a phoney-baloney world. The rules are phoney. The laws are phoney. I don't want to have anything to do with this lousy society. On pot, I'm happy." Jim argued as hard as he could: "Marc, many things are rotten, but we can change them if we don't give up before we start." Marc laughed in Jim's face: "You be a goody-goody, Jimmy boy, but just let me be." Jim and Marc drifted apart. One day Jim picked up a newspaper and saw Marc's frightened face on the front page. He had been picked up for possession of drugs. Jim's father looked at the newspaper and said, "Marc is a rotten kid, Jim." Jim replied, "No, dad, he's a sick kid. What I hold most against him is that he copped out." What did Jim mean? Do you agree? What else should Jim have said to Marc to try to straighten him out? Would it have been better if Jim had turned Marc in, before it was too late, to his parents, his rabbi, the police?

Jim has another friend in college named Scotty. Scotty believes pretty much as Jim does about the changes that are needed in our society. But Scotty doesn't agree with the way Jim goes about it. "You're a square, man," Scotty said. "You go puttering out to the Appalachian mountains to work in some foolish anti-poverty program. You think you can reform the system, make it better. But, man, the real scoop is that the whole system is corrupt, rotten, lousy. You have to tear it down. That's why I believe in revolution, not reform. We have to confront the power structure. Take over buildings on campus here. Force everybody to take sides. Stop the war by throwing our bodies in front of the induction centers; throwing our bodies in front of troop trains, so the wheels of war can't go around. You have faith in the system, you think you can improve it. But you're off your rocker man!"

To Jim, Scotty is also a "cop-out." Jim believes that Scotty doesn't have the patience to work for better conditions. Jim thinks Scotty would rather take dramatic or violent action than to solve problems. "I tell you, Scotty," Jim once said, "it is not hard to destroy. One

126

hand grenade can destroy a building. A hundred crazy kids like you could destroy a university. Maybe enough people like you can destroy this whole country. But what makes you think that something better would result? What would you put in its place? The great thing about America is that it is a free country. We are free to criticize. Free to organize in open ways to change conditions and solve problems. Free to set up political parties, to have demonstrations, to protest. But you are a wrecker, not a builder, and you and I are going to fight each other when we should be able to work together." And, in fact, Scotty and Jim are now on opposing sides in the struggles of students on the campus.

Jim and his parents do not understand each other very well. When he disappears into his room and starts to play his rock and folk records with such volume that the walls seem to tremble, his parents get irritable. "How can you stand that junk?" they ask. "And why does it have to blast our eardrums? Why don't you go out? Get some exercise!" Jim then gets angry and mutters, "You just don't understand me!" The truth is that they probably don't understand Jim anymore than he understands them. This is what everybody now calls the Generation Gap, or the Communication Gap. Do you see it in your house too?

Actually there has been such a gap in every generation. When Abraham smashed his father's idols at the very beginning of Jewish history, that was a generation gap. Parents and children have always been on different wave lengths. So the question is: Is it a bigger gap nowadays? Is it more serious nowadays? Is it more serious today than in the past? What do you think?

There is much evidence that the gap between the generations is more severe today than ever before. One evidence is the epidemic of drug use among young people, including early teenagers. Another evidence is the rebellion in hair, clothes, personal appearance; youngsters are saying they want to do their "own thing." Another is the student revolts, involving even grade-school children, protesting the ways which parents, teachers, and schools treat them. Another is the increasing number of children who run away from home and the frightening numbers who drop out of school. And of those youngsters who go on to finish school, few want to go into their father's business, many reject money-making as a prime goal, and most want to devote their lives to socially useful careers of serving other human beings — as social workers, anti-poverty workers, peace corpsmen, teachers, or government officials. This is all a reflection of the generation gap.

What it means is that the younger generation is reaching out for different values (what is really important) than their parents. Most youngsters grew up in comfort; so they never knew hunger or hardship. Their parents suffered through the Depression; so economic security is important to them. The parents are concerned with a good home, job, savings, security, future. But their children are concerned more with pleasure *now* than with a future, with meaning rather than comfort, with reaching out to other human beings rather than building a tight circle of security around their own families as a bulwark against a dangerous world. Many of the parents have given up on changing the world; but their children have not. Many of the parents want quiet and serenity and are afraid of turmoil; but their children seek excitement and feel things can't be changed without protest and even conflict. All this goes into the generation gap.

One interesting way to see the gap in action is to look over the lyrics of the songs which young people enjoy. Listen to the words of Dylan, Buckley, Donovan, Baez, the Beatles, and other records. What are these songs trying to say about the world? They are obviously condemning what they see as the phoniness of the adult society. They make fun of adults who belt a cocktail or two before dinner, who pop pep and other pills into their mouths, but who then fly into a rage when their child is caught experimenting with drugs. They make fun of an adult society which tells lies in business, in politics, in international relations, in advertising, and in their income taxes — and which gets unhinged by the frank honesty of children who insist on the truth, telling it like it is.

But not all the blame for the generation gap belongs with the parents. Young people contribute to it too. Somebody once said: "The present American generation of youth is great but it didn't read the minutes of the last meeting." Do you understand what was meant by this? It is possible for young people to be bright and smart without being wise. When youngsters act as if anybody over thirty years of age is useless, they cut themselves off from the experience of life and of history. Youngsters are often rude and arrogant, forgetting the commandment: "Honor your father and your mother." Youth does not have a monopoly on truth. And, to their surprise, there are millions of adults who share their vision of a better society and are knocking themselves out to achieve it. Youngsters need a touch of humility to match their energy.

The generation gap has a particular bite when it comes to Jews. For one thing, the adult generation of Jews was deeply scarred by living through Hitler's holocaust.

Youngsters cannot understand their parents emotions about this. Can you realize that there are many Jews alive today who actually feel guilty that they are alive — guilty that they didn't join their relatives and their martyred people in the gas chambers? And, likewise, adult Jews lived through the profound emotion of the miraculous birth in 1948 of the State of Israel, the state reborn after 2,500 years. But can youngsters, for whom there has always been an Israel, understand the tears and joys of their parents as they follow the news of Israel? Can the youngsters appreciate why their parents react so strongly to anti-Semitism, to attacks upon Israel, to war in the Middle East? The gap is deep and there is not too much that can be done about it.

There is another aspect of the youth revolt which bears strongly upon Jews. Because of our high regard for education, Jews are among the most educated groups in America. For America as a whole, 43 per cent of college-age youngsters are enrolled in college. But, for Jews, some 90 per cent of our college-age youngsters are in college. And, on the campuses, Jewish youngsters are strongly represented among the leaders and followers in campus movements for social reform. Why do you think this is?

One of the reasons is because of our Jewish religion. There are some religions which play down this world and talk about the world to come, the world after death. Judaism concentrates on this world. There are some religions which teach that people cannot really change things and that only God can bring justice, or peace, when He wants to do it. Judaism teaches that man is the partner with God in building a better world. Some religions teach that men are born bad; Judaism teaches that men are born good. Some religions teach that belief in God, or in Jesus, or in Buddha, is the most important thing a religious person has to do. But not Judaism. Judaism teaches that the most important thing is how a person lives, how he treats other human beings, whether he makes the world a better place than when he came into it. This is a religion of action. The prophets criticized those who thought that God was satisfied with religious services, holidays, rituals, and prayers. They insisted that God wants justice from man, fair dealings among people. The prophet Micah once said: "What does the Lord expect of you? Only to do justly, to love mercy, and to walk humbly with thy God."

Judaism is a religion of protest. It always has been. Abraham smashed the idols at great personal risk. Moses attacked the Egyptian who was enslaving his people. The Maccabees fought back against the Greek Syrians who took away their religious freedom. Esther and Mordecai resisted Haman's attempt to wipe out the Jewish people. Protest is an important principle of the Bible. "Thou shalt surely rebuke thy neighbor, and not bear sin because of him" (Lev. 19:17). What do you think that means? The rabbis once taught that Jerusalem was destroyed because the people of the city did not live up to their duty to criticize one another (Shabbat 119b). Likewise, one of the teachings of the Talmud is that "love which does not contain the element of criticism is not really love" (Bereshit Rabba 54:3). Protest, therefore, has a proud role in Jewish tradition. But, at the same time, protest which goes so far as to interfere with the rights of others, or is intended to harm other human beings, is bad. Protest should be intended to improve matters, not to make matters worse. Can you give examples of protest you regard as good and protest you regard as bad?

In a way, the active Jewish students on the college campuses may be living up to their religion better than some of the adults who attend services regularly and observe every Jewish holiday. What is funny about their actions is that many of these Jewish youngsters would deny that they are doing anything Jewish. But how else can we explain the high percentage of Jewish youngsters involved in demonstrations and protests and movements at Columbia, Berkeley, Wisconsin, Chicago, and many other campuses? Think back to the letter from Jim which opened this chapter. Jim is angry at his synagogue, but he is proud of the Jewish teachings that he learned there. Isn't it possible that what Jim learned about Judaism is what inspired him to give of himself in working for the poor people in Appalachia? Isn't it strange that the very people who probably taught Jim that Judaism is a way of life and a call to action are among the people who probably do not understand Jim now and may even think that Jim is a kooky radical of some kind for going off to live in such a way?

Too many of our homes are full of noise but lacking in real communication.

Television has had much to do with this. Families may watch together in dull silence like a group of robots; but conversation is usually not much more real than the commercials. Dinner time conversation may flit about the headline events of the day but, in most cases, does not deal with what is going on deep within the members of the family. When do we talk about ourselves, our problems, our fears, our hopes? Why is it that young people, in most cases, learn more about sex from the streets than from their parents? Why is it that movies are nowadays more frank than our own parents are with us? Why do so many parents wash their hands of their child's public and religious school education, leaving it completely to the teachers? Why is it so difficult for brothers and sisters to really talk to each other instead of playing games, teasing, joking, fighting, and laughing? Why do youngsters keep a problem steaming and growing inside themselves rather than sharing it with their parents? Is this true in your family? What can be done about it?

Some of the best folk music of the now generation reflects this problem of how people relate — or do not — to each other. Good examples are "The Sound of Silence" and "I Am a Rock" by Paul Simon of Simon and Garfunkle:

The Sound of Silence *

Hello darkness my old friend,
I've come to talk with you again,
Because a vision softly creeping,
Left its seeds while I was sleeping,
And the vision that was planted in my brain
    still remains
Within the sound of silence.

In restless dreams I walked alone
Narrow streets of cobblestone,
'Neath the halo of a street lamp,
I turned my collar to the cold and damp
When my eyes were stabbed by the flash of a
    neon light
That split the night
And touched the sound of silence.

And in the naked light I saw
Ten thousand people maybe more.
People talking without speaking,
People hearing without listening,
People writing songs that voices never shared

* ᶜ 1964, 1965 Charing Cross Music, Inc.

133

And no one dared
Disturb the sound of silence.

"Folks" said I, "You do not know
Silence like a cancer grows."
"Hear my words that I might teach you,
Take my arms that I might reach you."
But my words like silent raindrops fell,
And echoed in the wells of silence.

And the people bowed and prayed
To the neon God they made.
And the sign flashed out its warning
In the words that it was forming,
And the signs said "The words of the pro-
  phets are written on the subway walls
And tenement halls"
And whispered in the sound of silence.

I Am a Rock **

A winter's day in a deep and dark December,
I am alone.
Gazing from my window to the streets below,
On a freshly fallen silent shroud of snow,
I am a rock, I am an island.

I've built walls, a fortress steep and mighty
That none may penetrate,
I have no need of friendship, friendship cau-
  ses pain,
Its laughter and its loving I disdain,
I am a rock, I am an island.

Don't talk of love, well,
I've heard the word before,
It's sleeping in my memory;
I won't disturb the slumber
Of feelings that have died,

** ᶜ 1966 Charing Cross Music, Inc.

If I never loved I never would have cried.
I am a rock, I am an island.

I have my books and my poetry to protect me.
I'm shielded in my armor.
Hiding in my room,
Safe within my womb,
I touch no one,
And no one touches me,
I am a rock, I am an island.
And a rock feels no pain.
And an island never cries.

What do these songs mean? What is the writer trying to say? Is this a true picture of how people live and think, how they close themselves off from other people?
Have you listened to "A Day in the Life" by the Beatles? What are the Beatles telling us here? What is happening in each news item? What does it say about our work, about human nature?

Projects

1. Write a letter to Jim in answer to his.
2. Why do you think so many college youngsters are protesting on campus? What do they want?
3. Did you ever know anybody who thinks like Scotty? What would you say to him?
4. When the youngsters of today grow up and become parents, will they be any different from their parents? Will they communicate any better with their children?
5. A high proportion of the college activists are Jewish. Why do you think this is?
6. How do you explain why so many children experiment with drugs? How can this be dealt with? What should a school do with a student caught with marijuana in his possession?
7. Invite a college student from the congregation to talk to you about "student unrest."
8. Do you think young people should be represented on the Social Action Committee of the synagogue? How about the Board of the synagogue?

9. NFTY has a variety of exciting programs which stir tremendous enthusiasm in Jewish youth. Write to NFTY, 838 Fifth Avenue, New York, N. Y. 10021, about their Mitzvah Corps programs, Eisendrath-International-Exchange Program, Torah Corps, and other projects.

APPENDIX

A Dialogue on Social Action

This dialogue was first presented at the 43rd Biennial Assembly of the Union of American Hebrew Congregations, in Los Angeles, California, on February 13, 1955. It was written by Rabbi Eugene Lipman and Mr. Albert Vorspan.

Though the play can be used in many ways by various groups, it is urged primarily as a springboard for group discussion of the integral role that a social action program must play in the life of a synagogue. It can be followed by a general discussion of this type, or by discussions of specific areas of concern in the field of social justice, those alluded to in the script, and others as well.

The dialogue was revised with the help of Rabbi Balfour Brickner in order to keep the theme as contemporary and relevant as possible.

We hope that this brief dramatic presentation will be widely used to advance social action programs through which the ethical ideals of religion can be applied to the solution of the real problems of our society.

The stage setting consists of a lectern placed either stage center or to one side. The only props necessary are a spotlight directed at the lectern and a microphone off-stage for use by the person reading the part of the Voice of God.

The stage and room should be in darkness.

Soft, solemn chords serve as musical prelude. These chords in varying volume, should accompany the biblical quotations, as indicated in the script.

A spotlight hits — figure seated on stool, or at lectern, with a *Union Prayerbook* in his hand, obviously looking like any other Reform Jew involved in "the business of prayer."

137

MAN: "The Lord is near unto all who call upon Him, to all who call upon Him in truth." [*Union Prayerbook*, p. 116]

"Thou answered our prayers in the sight of all the living . . . . "

GOD: Who calls?

MAN: *(continues as though not hearing)* " . . . and thou satisfiest the desire of . . . "

GOD: Man!

MAN: What? *(as if to himself)* Who is disturbing me at this moment?

GOD: "I am *that* which I am."

I am *where* thou art.

MAN: What's going on here? Who are you? What do you want?

GOD: Have no fear, Man. No harm will come to you.

I speak to you now as I have spoken to your predecessors through eons of time —— I speak through your heart.

MAN: Ribbono Shel Olam! Master of the World.

GOD: Yes. The Eternal Presence. The God of your fathers.

MAN: But why? What are *You* doing here?

GOD: Are you surprised? Did you not just call Me in prayer?

MAN: Yes, but . . .

GOD: And I have answered.

MAN: Yes, I know, but . . .

GOD: But what?

MAN: But . . . well, frankly, I never expected to experience Your presence in so direct a fashion.

GOD: But you prayed.

MAN: Yes, I know, but You know how we feel about

138

prayer. It's just something we do — we're supposed to. It's a part of our "service" to You.

GOD: Is this how you serve Me?

MAN: It's part of it — a good part of it. Of course, we also have this temple. We built it for You; and let me tell You, it wasn't easy. A million dollars, in these times, is not to be sneezed at, God. Besides, an annual budget now in six figures is not a small matter.... God, don't You like our modern architecture?

GOD: *(somewhat disinterested and blasé)* There have been others, even more beautiful.

Is it built for Me or for you?

MAN: For You! A living monument to the living God.

GOD: A monument to Me? Ha! To Me ...

"The heavens declare the glory of God, the earth showeth His handiwork." [Psalms 19:2] Have you not said yourself that "the earth is My footstool"? [Isaiah 66:1] How can mortals praise Him when angels strive in vain?

... your own words, eh Man?

MAN: Yes, but what about all our activity: Sisterhood, Brotherhood, Youth groups, club programs, school, adult education, don't they count for something?

GOD: All quite lively. Indeed, quite lively, but, is it living?

MAN: But You *are* quite confusing. What *do* You want?

GOD: Come, come, Man, over here.

MAN: Where God? I can't see You. Where? I can't find You!

139

GOD: Ha! *(big, loud Ha!)* that figures. Here, over here.

Now, look, what do you see?

MAN: Why, that's my temple —

GOD: Is that all you see?

MAN: What else should I see? Oh.... You mean those old tenements. Yes, we worried about those before we built. Gosh, I'm sorry You think Your building is spoiled by its surroundings. *(music — solemn chords)*

GOD: *(angry)* "Look, ye blind, that ye may see ...
Here are people robbed and spoiled
They are snared in hovels,
And hid in slums;
They have come a prey, and none to rescue,
A spoil, with none to say restore." [Isa. 42:18ff.] *(end music)*

MAN: That's not quite fair. We didn't build those houses. One of our members owns a few of them, but that's not the temple's business. We don't own them. We have nothing to do with those people. They aren't our responsibility. *(music)*

GOD: "With their mouths and with their lips they honor Me,
But they have removed their hearts from Me,
And their fear of Me is a commandment learned by rote." [Isaiah 29:13]

So many thousands of times since Cain have men sought to excuse their inhumanity by asking: Am I my brother's keeper? And everyone of them has known My answer:
"Have we not all one father?
Hath not one God created us?

140

Why do we deal treacherously every man against his brother,
Profaning the covenant of our fathers?" [Malachi] *(end music)*

MAN: *(slowly)* I don't know.... It's all too much for me. Look God, I'm a simple, plain man. I do the best I can. I try to serve You, I try to love You, but I must tell You, God, it is hard, terribly hard to love You.

What do You expect of me? After all, I've a wife, children — Your gifts to me God.

Who can live by Your laws? What is it anyway? You command me to be holy. What is that? Who knows how to live daily according to such an unworldly precept?

GOD: " ... Ye shall be holy for I the Lord your God am holy. The wages of a hired servant shall not abide with thee all night until the morning.

" ... Thou shalt not curse the deaf, nor put a stumbling block before the blind.

" ... Thou shalt not respect the person of the poor, nor favor the person of the mighty; but in righteousness shalt thou judge thy neighbor. Thou shalt not go up and down as talebearer among thy people; neither shalt thou stand idly by the blood of thy neighbor; I am the Lord." [Lev. 19]

MAN: *(quietly)* "Before, I had heard of Thee by the hearing of the ear,
But now mine eye seeth Thee." [Job 42:5]

GOD: Say no more Man. Yet listen, for I have further burdens upon My spirit. Man, what do you see now?

141

MAN: That's the town hall, God.

GOD: Now listen, what do you hear?

MAN: Oh, that Luke Gillis. He's trying to force the school board to throw out all the books that deal with the United Nations. *(pause)* He says we're strong enough to lick all those foreigners put together.

GOD: Such words, too, have I heard many times, from the mouths of tyrants of many nations. How often have I watched My creatures, weak in courage and conviction, permit their souls to be taken captive. How often have men given up without a struggle the rights I gave them, the rights which are to make them but little lower than angels! *(music)* Fear not, O Man. "Be strong, and acquit yourselves like *men!* Acquit yourselves like men and fight!" [I Sam. 4:9] *(end music)*

MAN: But God, You don't know who this Gillis is. He's the President of the Pro-America Crusaders here in town. They have great power . . .

GOD: *(softly)* I know.

MAN: *(hardly taking breath from the last speech)* They've had school teachers fired; they so terrorized little Miss Larrabee, the librarian, that she got sick and resigned. They've smeared the minister down the street as a pro-communist because he preached against them in a sermon. . . . Gillis has an enormous following in this community. They say they're fighting against communism and for God . . . . How can we oppose them? Our temple can't afford to get mixed up with that kind of buzz saw. God, be practical. *(music)*

GOD: *(ironically)* Be practical. "Where wast thou when I laid the foundations of the earth? Declare, if thou hast the understanding. Who determined the measures thereof, if thou knowest? Or who stretched the line upon it? ...Hast thou commanded the morning since thy days began, and caused the dayspring to know its place? ...Hast thou entered into the spring of the seas? Or hast thou walked in the recesses of the deep? ...Hast thou surveyed unto the breadths of the earth? Declare, if thou knowest." [Job 38] O Man, My universe, My law, My will — these are practical. *(end music)*

MAN: God, let me be. I've got to think.

GOD: There will be much time for you to think. But first, come here yet again, I would show you still another burden. What do you see?

MAN: Why I know him. That's Mr. Prince, the black minister.

GOD: What else do you see?

MAN: But ... how can it be ... that's me!

GOD: Yes, Man. Do you remember?

MAN: *(silence)* Y-e-e-es. I had just given Mr. Prince some money, from a few of us, to help him organize a committee to plan desegregation in our schools.

GOD: That was good. Is that all?

MAN: Well ... No-o-o. ... Mr. Prince thanked me, and then he said. "Your temple could add great strength to our work." I — I — I said, "Mr. Prince, we were glad to give you this money. Some of us believe in your cause. But I'm sure you will understand that our temple as such cannot be involved. Our temple must stick to religion."

GOD: Religion? What is your temple for? What do your prayers mean? *(music)* "Bring no more vain oblations;
It is an offering of abomination unto Me;
New moon and Sabbath, the holding of con-vocations.
I cannot endure iniquity along with the sol-emn assembly.
... When ye make many prayers, I will not hear;
Your hands are full of blood.
... Cease to do evil;
Learn to do well.
Seek justice, relieve the oppressed, remove the shackles from the minds and hearts of men."
[Isaiah 1:13-17] *(end music)*

MAN: A million dollar temple! A thousand families. A rabbi! Is it enough? Is it even a beginning? For what *do* we stand? *To* what do we stand up and say: Here am I, send me!
O God, how can we serve You better?

GOD: *(very softly)* It hath been told thee O Man what is good and what the Lord doth require of thee. Only to do justly, to love mercy, and to walk humbly with thy God.

ASSOCIATION FOR JEWISH YOUTH
AJY HOUSE, 50 LINDLEY STREET
E1 3AX   Tel. 01-790 64?? 9